Stairway

to

Heaven

David A. Drew

Cover Photograph by Bryan Leslie

ACKNOWLEDGEMENTS

Special thanks to Maureen Singleton,

my wife Jane and to all my friends

both on earth and in the spirit world

for all their help and support.

INTRODUCTION

The End of the World

INTRODUCTION

I would like to say a few words by way of introduction to the author of this work. It would be misleading for the reader to jump to any preconceived conclusions about this man, before reading the ensuing pages.

David Drew, if you attempted to give him a title at all, would I suppose be classed as a spiritual medium and healer, but in truth, this label does not do this man justice. There is much more to him than that.

There are many mediums throughout the world, but it must be said that the author of this book is surprisingly unique. In recent years, the many books written by various psychics have been helpful in creating the snowballing interest in 'life after death'. The subject is fascinating to everyone, but this has resulted in questions being raised that, until now, have remained unanswered. This book goes beyond the messages from your grandmother. It takes the subject one step further and dares to explain in simple, earthly language, matters which are not of this world.

David has astounded people all of his life, not only with his remarkable psychic powers, but with his immense spiritual knowledge. He has been called a 'twentieth century prophet', a 'miracle worker', and a 'messenger'. However, David is reluctant to call himself anything. He dislikes 'pigeon holes', but rather prefers to allow individuals to decide for themselves.

Over the years, David has of course brought comfort and hope to thousands of people. He passes on messages from those in what he calls the spirit world, gives advice on life and conducts spiritual healing; bringing about cures and / or relief to countless sufferers of all kinds of ailments. However, this is by no means all that this man does. He says that his most important message is for all people, he has a message for you!

David travels extensively throughout Britain, and indeed other countries, with the aim of reaching as many people he possibly can with the important message which he says he has 'for the world'. David conducts public demonstrations in large theatres, halls, and other public places, where he passes on messages from those in the spirit world and invites questions from audiences. It is a rule of his that he will speak anywhere where people wish to hear him. In the past, he has spoken in bars and even discotheques, as well as churches and theatres. Whatever the venue, David's genuine down to earth, yet light-hearted style is always well received. Increasing demand has meant that he also works extensively on television and radio throughout the world.

It is David's intent that this book be easily understandable, and should contain the answers to many of your questions on life after death, reincarnation, dreams, astral travel, spiritual healing, heaven and hell, religion and even the meaning of life, but, more importantly than this, he is giving you the benefit of his unique spiritual knowledge in showing you how you may climb that steep staircase to heaven.

And how did David acquire this spiritual knowledge? How could he know all the answers? The answer may surprise you.

David actually recalls his time in spirit before he was born. He speaks about the spirit world with authority because he has been there and, which is more to the point, has clear recollection of this. He has not a faith, but a precise knowledge of God and his laws.

David Drew may be the author of this book, but the words come from the highest spirit realms. These words will change the lives of those who accept them, and in turn this may change the world for the better. Only then will the writer's job be complete.

Ever since the beginning of time, prophets have been ridiculed, mocked and scorned, even by the Church. David is no exception. Sceptics have called him crazy, orthodox religious leaders accuse him of being the work of the devil and extremists try to put a stop to his work.

Those who listen to this man are convinced he is quite sane, those who are comforted and healed through him are certain he is no demon. Madman, Satan or saviour? You must decide, but whatever conclusions you settle upon, you must surely agree that David Drew has remarkable, original and logical answers to all the questions you could ever ask about this life, past lives and the life to come.

Jane E. Drew.

Chapter 1

Life After Death

In the River Thames, there lived two fish. As they swam along, content in their little world, one said to the other, 'I have heard that up above us there is a land with beautiful greenery and huge buildings. They say that in this place creatures do not need water in order to breathe and that it is huge and magnificent.' The other fish eyed him in disbelief, 'Don't be ridiculous! How could these things be true? Do you know anyone who has ever been to this place?' His friend thought for a moment. It was true to say that, from time to time, fish disappeared from the river, but he could not prove that they had gone to this land. If they had, they had never come back to tell him, so he remained silent. 'I thought not!' gloated his companion whilst gulping down a worm, 'I shall never believe what I do not see with my own eyes!' No sooner had he spoken than a sharp hook caught hold of his lip and whisked him sharply upwards through the water and out into the air. As he flew toward the bright light, he saw huge buildings and a vast blue sky. He saw strange creatures flying in the air and still more walking on the ground in this amazing new world. 'My friend was right after all!' he thought, 'If only I could go back and tell him so!' Of course it was too late.

This little story illustrates that whilst confined to this material, physical world of ours, it can be difficult for the blinkered mind to accept anything other than the world it can see.

There was the time when people believed that the world was flat! In those days, countries like America were the 'unknown', and when people spoke of the earth being round, or people living in distant lands, they were laughed at in much the same way as those who believe in the spirit world may be ridiculed today.

However, believers and sceptics alike, at some time in their lives all ponder over the question, 'is there life after death, and if so, what happens to us upon physical death?'

If anything is certain in this life, it is that we are all going to die. Some will say, 'When we are dead we are dead. That is it! The end – nothing!' I feel so sorry for these people who think this way. What do they have to look forward to? What can they work towards? They must wonder why we have a life at all, and what a shock for them when one day, they 'wake up' dead!

Others may have a faith or religious conviction that there is a happier life to come, but what kind of a life? Where is this other world, and is it really better than this world? Many orthodox religions believe, one way or another, that death is not the end, so if it is right to believe in an after life, then what is wrong with trying to find out what really happens upon physical death? Death is a journey which everyone must make. As with any journey, it is right and proper to discover as much as you can about your destination. If you were travelling to a foreign land, you would wish to find out all you could about that country before embarking on your journey. You would wish to know what it is like, what were the people like, how you could get there, what the climate was like and what you would need to take with you.

There is nothing to fear in death itself. It is, in fact, a most natural act which everyone does and no-one likes to talk about – rather like going to the toilet, don't you think? Of course, the cause of death can be worrying. No-one wishes to experience a long, slow, painful death, but the actual act of dying is just a simple passing, rather like walking into the next room. How do I know it is as simple as that? I have experienced it myself on a few occasions. How do I know there is a world beyond this? I have been there!

You may have a belief that there is a country called China, but how do you know for certain, and how can you know what it is like? You can find out all about China by listening to someone who has lived there. Listen to me when I tell you of the world to come… I have lived there!

Why is it that people fear death? Maybe it is because people are afraid of the unknown? And to most people, death is the unknown. By discovering more about the world to come you can, to a greater degree, eliminate that fear. Also, one may fear the separation from their loved ones, but by accepting that in reality, our loved ones who have gone before us are never very far away, that fear may also be erased.

When we mourn at the passing of a loved one, who are we really grieving for? Is it the loved one or ourselves? They are now living on in another world, leaving us behind. It is surely ourselves, in our own loneliness that we grieve for.

Before I explain more about what happens upon physical death, it is important to explain how we are all 'made up'. We all consist of a physical body and a spirit body. The physical body is what I call the 'vehicle' which we need whilst we are here on the earth. When we pass over, however, we no longer have any use for this physical body, which can then be disposed of, and so it is buried or burnt. Our spirit, however, our real self lives on.

You see, I wish you to understand that we are spirit now. We do not die and become spirit; we are spirit, encased in a physical body for our duration here on earth.

When a diver goes down deep into the ocean, he needs to wear a diving suit, and when we are on the earth, we too need to wear an appropriate 'outer suit'. This is our physical body. When the diver is pulled up into the sunshine, he no longer needs his heavy attire, and so he discards it. When we pass to spirit, we no longer need our heavy attire, our physical body, and it is this which we cast off. Our real self, our spirit, lives on, and just as our physical body needs fuel in the form of food and drink, our spirit body requires fuel of a different kind. It needs spiritual knowledge and understanding.

The earth is just one plane of existence, of which there are many, and it is the only plane which demands that we wear this suit. It is the manner in which we live our lives on this earth which determines the plane of existence we will go to upon our passing.

We are only renting our space on God's earth, and the way to pay our rent is by contributing to other people, and it is in this way that we earn the reward, or retribution, to come.

You never stop learning, but do not wait until you pass over before beginning to spiritually develop. Start now! The more you can learn and develop whilst here on earth, the higher and better home you will have in spirit.

Always remember that death is just a simple journey, and one which we must all make. As with any journey, preparations have to be made. We can begin to prepare now, by realising the reason we are here on earth. We are here to learn, to experience, to develop spiritually and to make our contributions. Each of us have something to contribute to this earth, and the people on it, before it is time for us to pass to the worlds beyond.

Chapter 2

What Happens Upon Death

The actual act of dying, as I mentioned earlier, is nothing at all to fear. It is the most natural process in the world, as simple as passing from one room to the next.

Upon physical death, the spirit leaves the earthly body to being a new and exciting life in the spirit world. The spiritual and physical bodies are joined by what is known as the 'silver cord'. Upon death, the spirit leaves the physical body and this silver cord is severed. Actual death does not occur until the breaking of this cord.

You may say that the entering and departing of this life are very similar. We come into the world at the cutting of a cord. And we leave the world at the cutting of a cord. As the umbilical cord is broken when we commence this life, so the silver cord is broken as we commence the next, the major difference being that the latter is considerably easier and not nearly so messy!

The silver cord is, in appearance, rather like a length of rope, which brilliantly shines and radiates a pure, silvery blue light. You may, on occasions, have heard or read about someone who 'died' for a while, maybe on the operating table, and was brought 'back to life'.

This is what is known as a 'near death experience'. It must, however, be made clear that 'death' itself did not take place in such cases. What, in fact, happens is this.

The spirit leaves the body, but remains joined to it by the silver cord. People who have encountered these experiences report such events as looking down on their own bodies, travelling through a tunnel of light and possibly meeting up with family or friends, long since passed over. When their physical body is resuscitated, however, and the doctors manage to make their heart beat again, the spirit returns to the body and life on earth continues for them. If, on the other hand, the silver cord is broken, this permanently releases the spirit, and there is no possible way on earth that they could be brought back to life again.

In this day and age, we have wonderful life supporting machines which do a good job, but if the silver cord has been severed, then there is no way that the person could live again in that body. The machine may well inflate the lungs, and keep the heart beating, but if the spirit has gone, then the shell is empty. The person is no longer there. At this point, the body is what is known as 'brain stem dead'.

Upon physical death, when the spirit body is lifted out of the physical body, you may see relatives or friends who have passed on before you. They come to greet you and to help you. Slowly, you begin to adjust to life in this new world.

The condition of the physical body, or the way in which we die, can affect our mental attitude upon our passing. For instance, an elderly gentleman who has led a good life may slip in and out of his body, still joined by the silver cord. His spirit may visit friends and relatives in the spirit world, who come close to him to assist him during his own transition. He may fall in and out of sleep state, and during physical consciousness report that he has seen his past family members. As his spirit travels between these states of physical and spiritual, the silver cord will slowly become thinner and thinner, until it finally breaks, whereupon the gentleman passes to spirit, and his physical body dies.

Now, in contrast, where a young man dies instantly, perhaps as a result of an accident, the silver cord can be instantly cut, and it is not unusual on these tragic occasions, for the young man not to immediately realise what has happened. Indeed, he may 'get up' and think that he has had a miraculous escape. He may speak to those around him, and wonder why they do not acknowledge him. He may ask his parents why they are crying, not understanding what has happened or why they do not hear him. In such a case as this, the young man would have to be helped by those in spirit, and this could be a long and difficult process.

In cases where someone dies as a result of a long and traumatic illness, perhaps in hospital, then upon passing they can find themselves in what are known as 'spirit hospitals', where they slowly recover. Here, they are helped to adjust to their new life, and realise that they are now free from any physical illness. I will talk more of spirit hospitals in the pages which follow.

Immediately upon your passing to spirit, you will go to what I call 'no man's land'. Here you will spend a while adjusting to your new circumstance. Many people are very confused when they pass, as they have little spiritual knowledge or understanding. They must come to realise what has happened to them. It can be quite a shock to some people when they wake up dead! They must begin to accept that they are spirit, not physical. They will see that they have lost any physical disabilities, they are free of any pain and they have much to learn.

Too many people pass over with very wrong preconceived ideas because of their religious (or prejudiced) upbringing. You see, there are not one thousand and one different religions in the spirit world. Of course, some people are convinced that there is no life after death at all. What a shock it is to these people. They are very confused!

When you pass over to spirit, you leave your physical body behind. You then have to become accustomed of not carrying the weight of your body around with you.

Immediately upon passing, you may see your departed relatives or friends, who come to help you to adjust. Then comes the part which most people dread. At this point, your helpers in spirit will analyse with you every event in your earthly life: all your thoughts, words and deeds. You will be shown just where you went wrong and how your actions affected other people. It is at this point that your new home will be determined. You will go to a place of existence where everyone is at the same stage of development as yourself, and there you will continue to learn.

So please, do not look upon death as the end. When the caterpillar thinks it is the end of the world, the master knows it is turning into a butterfly!

Chapter 3

The Spirit World

In the spirit world, there are many planes of existence, and the manner in which you have lived your life on earth determines which of these spiritual planes you will go to.

Of course, the higher the plane, the better it is. If you have lived a very spiritual earthly life, then you will go to a higher spiritual plane than if you had not, but whichever plane you go to, you can, by learning and understanding, earn your progression to higher levels.

At this point, I would like to clarify that when I speak of higher or lower spiritual planes, I do not actually mean to say that these places are up in the sky or down in the ground. I use these words merely for ease of understanding. The various planes are, of course, dimensions away, on different vibrations. People often have difficulty in relating to this, and so I explain in simple terms which people may understand.

From no man's land, you will travel in an instant to your new home in spirit, the place where you deserve to be. Each plane higher than the earth is a nicer, more spiritual place. The next plane up from the earth is known as the 'astral' plane. Here, the minds of people still tend to think upon a material rather than a spiritual level. For this reason, they may live in houses and wear clothing, much the same as they did on the earth plane. These things are created by the power of thought.

Animals also have an afterlife, and if it is your wish that a long since departed pet dog be with you, it may be so.

If however you were to progress to the high spirit planes, you would find things rather different. Here, people have a much greater understanding and are far more spiritual. They no longer feel the need for material possessions, such as houses, and rather than clothing as we know it, they are adorned in robes of various bright colours, which upon inspection are found to be hazes of glowing, coloured light rather than any kind of physical material.

There is no language barrier here, because there is no speech as we know it. People on these planes communicate by means of telepathy, or thought transference.

It would be impossible for me to describe in earthly words the beauty of these lands. You could not imagine such wonders. This place is like nothing you have ever seen on earth. In a finite mind, it is also difficult to understand that there is no time or space as we know it in the spirit world. Time and distance are very different there, and you are able to travel what we would consider to be great distances in an instant all with the power of thought.

All things, however, must have an opposite. How could you appreciate light unless you had known dark? How would you know large unless you had seen small? How could you know what was good if there was no bad? All things have an opposite, and if you can be promoted from the earth to higher, brighter planes, so then you can be demoted, down to what I describe as the 'dark, grey pits'! This plane is lower than the earth plane, and you may be surprised to learn just how many people fall through that 'trap door', straight down to this dark, grey, miserable abode. Here you see those who have not lived spiritual lives wandering around, heads bowed low, sent down there as a result of their sinful lives. If only people on earth could take a glimpse into this cesspit, I am sure they would change their lifestyles. Would you believe that more people go down to the 'pits' upon passing, than those who float up to the high spirit realms?

There are, of course, some people who perhaps prefer the dark. Like a burglar prefers the dark. Burglars are afraid of the light for fear of being caught. These people have all their selfish, sinful lives hanging around them, dragging them further and further down. Only those who have inhabited the high spirit realms are allowed to travel down to these dark grey areas, because those from the high spirit realms are protected. No harm can come to them. However, if those on the astral plane were allowed to venture down, it could happen that they too would get dragged down into this bottomless pit.

Do not make the mistake of thinking that in these dark grey areas there are only murderers and evil people as such. There are people down there who you may not expect! There are people from history who you perhaps think did not lead such an evil life, but be sure your sins will find you out. When anyone passes over to spirit, there is no hiding place. All your thoughts, words and actions on the earth plane are revealed for all to see. Everyone can see you for what you are, and people who have perhaps not been found out during their earthly life will certainly be found out when they pass to spirit!

There are souls there who are filled with the torture of remorse, more bitter than anything you can possibly imagine. They wander around aimlessly in the dark. They wear dark drab hooded cloaks with their head bowed in shame, and they wander around with no direction. If people could only visit these places and see the areas that I am trying to describe to you, I know that they would change their ways.

There are those in these dark grey areas who repent. As I have said, progression is open to everyone, even these poor unfortunate souls. If we can help them and manage to get them out of this pit of darkness and despair, what they must then do is have another life on the earth plane. They are given the chance to try again. However, as I have said, there are those who 'yo yo' up and down. They come from the dark pit, they are reincarnated and have a life on the earth plane, where they do not learn and go straight back down again. Up and down I have seen these people go because they are having difficulties in grasping simple lessons, simple spiritual truths.

Listen to our words from spirit, and there is every chance that fewer people will be leaving the earth plane and going down to this dark, grey, dismal pit.

The earth is in darkness when compared to the high spirit planes, but it is brilliant when contrasted with the 'pits'.

There are people down there, who are filled with torture and remorse, and they must work towards their own salvation, but the beauty is that progression is open to everyone.

Those on higher spirit planes do travel down to visit and help those on lower planes, but those on the lower planes cannot go up to visit. They must earn their progression by learning and understanding. Rather like the slide in a children's playground, it is hard to climb up the ladder, but easy to slide down. When those from the high spirit realms travel down to visit the different planes, they must speak to the people at their own level. They speak to those on the earth plane in very, very simple terms so that they may understand and not become confused. The more they speak, however, the more questions are raised, and it is always their fear that earthly minds will not comprehend what they are saying. Valuable words, like seeds, can fall on stony ground.

The earth plane is the only plane of existence where there are people sharing the same plane who are on different spiritual levels, and this is the only plane where people have come from various different levels, and will be going to various different levels.

For example, if we number the major planes and call the pits number one, the earth number two the astral number three and so on, those on number three the astral, are working towards and can go to number four. From number four, they work towards and can go to number five, and so on. In other words, they may steadily progress forwards, one plane at a time.

Those from the pits must also come up to the next plane, the earth plane, before they can further progress. That is to say they must be reincarnated and have another life here.

On the earth plane, however, people do not know what they are working towards. They may leave this plane and go to the astral or to the pits, but it is also possible for them to go directly to number six or number seven without touching the others.

This earth plane is also unique in that we share it with people who have chosen to come here from all different planes. There are those here whose previous existence was in the pits, those whose previous existence was on the astral, and those whose previous existence was fairly high in the spirit world, maybe plane number six or even seven.

In the spirit world, as I mentioned previously, those from higher planes are able to travel down through the lower planes in order to visit, whereas those on the lower planes cannot travel upwards without first earning their progression.

Therefore, if your husband, who has led a spiritual life, passes before you, he will learn and progress even further in the spirit world. When the time comes for you to pass over, if your life has not been so spiritual, you may find yourself on a plane lower than his. He may come down to greet you upon your passing, and he is able to make the journey downwards to visit you from time to time, but not until you have progressed to his level will you be together on the same plane.

It is true to say, however, that it is possible for the husband, in such a case, to voluntarily postpone any further progression in order to wait for his wife to join him, whereupon they may progress together.

When two people have been very close and one passes over to spirit, it can happen that the remaining partner grieves too much for too long and in so doing inadvertently holds their loved one back from progression. Grieving acts rather like a magnet, and makes the person in spirit reluctant to advance. If they could only realise that the further the can progress, the easier it is to come back and visit their loved ones back on the earth. Grief is, of course, a natural reaction upon losing someone close, but prolonged grief can be detrimental to all concerned.

By living a spiritual and unselfish earthly life, and by gaining spiritual knowledge whilst here on earth, we can all work towards happiness in a bright new world to come. Everyone lives on after death as life is eternal, but just what kind of a place you will go to is entirely up to you.

When all of your earthly life is analysed, every event, every action, every word and every thought, then each sin will act rather like a brick around your neck, weighing your down. Each unselfish act to help others will act rather like a balloon to help raise you up. Think on this for a moment. When your time comes, will you be surrounded by bricks or balloons?

Chapter 4

Reincarnation

The whole reason for us having a life on the earth is to learn, to develop, to understand and to experience. It is in this way that we spiritually progress.

There are so many things which we must experience and understand. The earth is our training ground. It is here that we may experience and learn. Your life here is like a day at school. You have much to learn, and when you have completed your work and the bell goes, it is good to go home. But just as we cannot learn all our lessons in one day at school, so we cannot learn all we need to know in one life time, and so it is that we have many, many lives here on earth.

Every one of us was in the spirit world before we were born. When in spirit, one reaches a point when we realise which lessons we need to learn and which experiences we must go through in order to spiritually progress. It is usually easier to learn by personal experience, and so it is decided that we should have another life on the earth plane. Who our parents should be and the conditions surrounding our earthly life are predetermined.

For example, if you have lived a life on earth in which you wanted for nothing, perhaps born to rich parents, educated at the best schools and given everything you could desire, then it is difficult for you to understand what poverty is like. You cannot possibly know what it is like to go hungry or struggle unless you experience it for yourself. You need to learn that life should not be about material wealth, big houses and fat bank balances, and so you are reborn, perhaps to a starving family in the third world.

When you pass over to spirit again, the chances are that your priorities will have shifted somewhat, and that you will have learned this lesson.

It is, of course, impossible to take material possessions accumulated here on earth with you into the next world, but there is one thing that you can acquire in this world and still carry with you to the next. This is spiritual knowledge. We must all get our priorities right and look to the long term. Spiritual treasures are the things we should accumulate. Sooner or later, we must all learn to live a spiritual rather than a material life.

It can take some people a very long time to learn these very simple lessons, and so they will have many, many incarnations, and that is to say they will come back time and time again until they have learned. It can be extremely frustrating and will certainly hold up spiritual progression if people have to keep coming back to learn the same lessons because they have not understood.

We all have our own free will, and no-one can be forced into having another life on earth. If, however, someone refuses the opportunity, then their progression can be seriously impaired.

A common fear harboured by believers in reincarnations is that when they pass over to spirit, their loved ones –

be it grandmother, husband, wife or child – may have already reincarnated, and so they will not be able to see them when they pass. This is an unfounded fear; however, as it may take many hundreds of years our time, before a person is ready to be born again onto the earth. Your loved ones will still be in the spirit world when it is your turn to pass through the veil called death, and it is possible to be reunited with them.

It is possible also to have some small insight into your own past life. Have you ever been somewhere that you know you have not visited before, and yet you feel that you are familiar with the surroundings? You hear quite frequently of people experiencing this. It is commonly referred to as déjà vu. This can be due to a number of things, and one of them is that you could have lived there in a previous lifetime. Have you ever met someone for the first time, and yet you feel that you know them? Or perhaps you have experienced love at first sight. This can be explained by the fact that you were with this person in a previous life, or indeed in the spirit world.

These experiences are glimpses into a past life which anyone may encounter from time to time. People do not ordinarily remember their past incarnations, as everyone begins this life with a clean slate. I am often asked by curious friends, 'Tell me who I was in a previous life?' and my answer is always the same. 'What good would it do you? It is not important.' We should be more concerned with this life. We cannot change the past, but we can determine our future. It is how we live our lives here and now which is important.

In conclusion, we must welcome all experiences, good and bad, and learn all we can from them. In times of trouble, remember that God drives us into deep water, not to drown us, but to cleanse us. All things are for a purpose. We sometimes need to go through difficult experiences in order to be better people, with more understanding as a result of them. Remember, tears which we shed through difficulties will one day turn into pearls of wisdom.

Chapter 5

Your Higher Self

I would like, at this stage, to explain a little about the 'mind'.

Now, let me make it clear that the mind and the brain are not one and the same. Your brain is a physical organ which is part of your earthly body. This, of course, decays upon physical death. However, you have one mind and one spirit which make up your real self. Whilst the 'physical body' and 'brain' is mortal, the real you is immortal, that is to say it has always been and will always be. It is simplicity itself. Your physical body has a brain; your spirit houses your mind.

Throughout your early life, everything that you experience is registered by your brain, which transfers all the information to your mind, via the silver cord. When you pass to spirit, you will recall all of your earthly life, because everything that you ever do, say or even think will have passed along the silver cord to your mind, which is part of your spirit or true self.

The information stored by the mind may, of course, be right or wrong. You decide which information to accept as truth and which to reject as untruth. The rejected information sinks into the depth of your mind as you will not expect this to be useful to yourself or others. The information kept to the forefront of your mind is what you consider to be goodness and truth which hopefully will be useful to yourself and to whomever you will pass the information onto. To accept or reject the wrong information can be quite disastrous.

It is true that we have one spirit and one mind, but we may, over many centuries, have inhabited many earthly bodies. Whilst in the body, it is usual to only use a small part of your mind, the part which registers your earthly experiences. The whole mind is what I call your 'higher self'. Here you have endless fields of knowledge which has been gained through all your previous lives and existences in spirit. Once you have learned to, you can 'tap into' or draw from this vast ocean of knowledge.

You may, at some time during your life, find yourself in a very difficult situation that you simply do not know how to cope with. Suddenly the solution, or what you must do, just seems to come to you. This is because that knowledge is there in your higher self, maybe put there during a previous lifetime, and this knowledge was able to travel via the silver cord back from the mind to your present brain. With practice, teaching and much patience, you can develop this ability to tap into your higher self whenever you want to, but I could not explain in a few words what may take many, many years to achieve.

When you pass to spirit and eventually reach the high spirit realms, you will become not just one person but an accumulation of all your lives, with all the knowledge you ever had.

Allow me to tell you a little story by way of example. Once upon a time, a little baby girl was born in Italy. Her name was Maria. She encountered many different experiences throughout her earthly life, and at the age of sixty seven, she passed over to spirit where, of course, she was accountable for all of her earthly actions. Maria continued to learn her lessons in the spirit world. She was shown what she did right and what she did wrong, and three hundred years later, it was decided that should have another life on the earth plane.

She was reborn as a baby boy in Paris. His name was Pierre. At the age of just twenty five, Pierre was tragically killed in a mountaineering accident. He passed to spirit and his life was analysed. Although his life was short, he had made many mistakes and had much to learn. He began to learn and progress in the spirit world, and two hundred years later, he was reincarnated.

In England, a baby girl, named Anne, was born. She grew up and passed to spirit as an old woman in her eighties. Anne had many lessons to learn and experiences to go through. In spirit, her life was analysed; this time she was not reincarnated, but rather progressed further in the spirit world. She learned well and was promoted to the higher spirit realms, where became, no longer just Anne, but an accumulation of all her lives. She became, not one person, but a combination of Maria, Pierre and Anne, that is to say her complete higher self.

Whilst here in a physical world, it can be very difficult to comprehend this. I have simplified it as far as possible, but not until you experience it for yourself will you completely understand.

Now, let us talk for one moment about Maria. Remember her? She was the Italian lady who died aged sixty seven. The lessons that she learned, both on the earth and in spirit after her passing, would be her 'higher self'. This higher self, this store of knowledge would remain deep within her mind when she reincarnated as Pierre in France. The higher self of Maria would be with Pierre throughout his life, and he could learn, as everyone can, to tap into this higher self if need be.

Now, when Pierre passed to spirit, the lessons he learned on the earth and in spirit would combine with the lessons Maria learned.

And so it is that when he was born again as Anne, she would have with her the higher self which consisted of the accumulation of lessons learned by Maria and Pierre, both on earth and in spirit, and so it goes on. This is a very simple example. It can, of course, be much more complicated.

As you walk this pathway of life, the forefront of your mind is like a rucksack which you carry on your back. Along the way, you can collect valuable information and store it in this rucksack, whilst knowledge which you consider to be rubbish is cast aside. It is, however, possible to pick up rubbish by mistake, and throw it in your rucksack, so do take care. Many people, I fear, are walking along with much trash in their rucksacks. Now is the time to spring clean! Clear out any rubbish your higher self may be holding onto, and replace it with clean, pure spiritual knowledge.

Chapter 6

My Mission Here on Earth

Most people can remember their childhood. Can you remember when you were a small child? The interesting or amusing events you will perhaps remember more clearly. Do you recall being a baby lying in your pram? Can you think back even further than that? What about the time you spent in your mother's womb? In quiet meditation, try to remember; believe me, it is possible!

Can you remember the years before you were born? This is not as crazy as it sounds. Life is eternal, that does not just mean in front of us, but also behind us. Everyone was in spirit before they were born onto the earth. We are spirit, we have always been spirit and we will always be spirit. There is no beginning and no end. This earthly life, of course, has a beginning and an end, but one's existence does not. In this finite body of ours, it is impossible to imagine being infinite but we are. It may surprise you if I say that I am able to clearly remember my existence in spirit before the earthly life I now have. I remember being in spirit and looking down on the earth, rather like watching a football match from the stands, looking down onto the pitch. From the comfort of your seat, it looks so easy. You can observe when someone does something wrong. You may shout out, 'Pass the ball', or other such instructions.

So it was with me. I could see clearly from my home in spirit, how people were making such a mess of their lives. Some people were being led in all sorts of different directions, every way it seemed, except the right one. The world began to look very dark, people were getting lost and confused. I saw so many people, thousands upon thousands every year, passing over to spirit without any spiritual knowledge at all. Needless to say, these people continued to be lost and confused in spirit. I was filled with sadness, dismay and despair.

I remember the outbreak of the First World War in August 1914. This war known as the 'Great War' cost the lives of over ten million people in just four years. We in spirit were kept very busy helping all those people whose earthly lives had been prematurely cut short.

In spirit, one does not have a physical body, but one does have a clear mind, feelings and emotions. It was indeed very sad to see God's children fighting one another, killing one another, hating one another. All we could do was to try to influence the minds of people, but everyone possesses their own free will.

It seems that people do not learn their lessons. Shortly after the First World War followed the second. By the end of the Second World War it was clear that people had lost their spirituality. People began to rebuild their lives, with the emphasis on material possessions and wealth.

What was happening to God's children on God's earth? From spirit, we were filled with sorrow for the poor, unfortunate people who seem to have no real direction or purpose in their lives. I have said before, there are many planes of existence in spirit, higher ones each more beautiful than lower ones, but there is also what I regularly refer to as the pits. This plane of existence is not at all pleasant; a dark, cold, damp place where everything looks grey, where you see people who have not led a spiritual life walking about aimlessly in their misery, a condition brought about by their own misguided earthly lifestyles. More and more people were passing from this earth, straight down to this awful existence, and things were not improving. Indeed, in the past decade alone, millions of people made the transition from this world to the next. Seventy five per cent of those people have gone down to the pits, twenty per cent have managed to reach the astral and only five per cent have gone higher than this.

Whilst in spirit, many years ago, we could see the way things were going. Something had to be done. It was decided that I should come down and have yet another life on earth, to spread a very important message to all peoples everywhere. A message of life and spiritual truths. Here I am.

I am but a signpost, pointing the way. I cannot make people do anything. I cannot make people believe the things I say, but it is my task to give people the opportunity to listen to the spiritual truths, they must themselves decide which way to go.

Too many people were passing over and trying to use the excuse 'But how was I to know how to live my life. How could I know that I was doing wrong?' I take away that excuse for people going wrong. When people who have listened to what I have to say pass over to spirit, they can be asked, 'How did you get lost? We even gave you a signpost!' In this life of mine, it is of the utmost importance that I reach as many people as I possibly can in the time I have. The way in which to do this in this day and age is to use the available media, which is why my task is concentrated in the areas of television, radio, newspapers, magazines, public demonstrations, lectures and perhaps most importantly, books.

You see, there is to be a wonderful party on the high spirit planes, a place where only the most spiritual of people may go. I am sending out the invitations. On the reverse of the invitation is a map, showing you how to get there. This is as much as I can do for you. I cannot carry you there. I cannot drive a coach and take you there, and neither can I drag you kicking and screaming if you do not wish to go. I have an invitation for you and I am showing you the way. I hope to see you there, but take care. The road is a dangerous one and it is too easy to stumble or lose your way. Listen carefully to my instructions. I am showing you how to climb that steep stairway to heaven. Can you imagine setting out on a long journey to an unfamiliar destination? You would need a map and signs along the way. How could you possibly get there if you had no map and there were no signs? It would be impossible. All people everywhere are travelling on a journey. I am offering you a map, please read it. I am pointing out the signs, please watch for them. If people choose not to read the map I give them, and they ignore the signs I show them, is it any wonder they get lost?

The people of this world are like two men walking through the desert without water. They stumble upon an oasis and converse. 'Ah,' they may say, 'But is it a mirage?' 'Ah,' they may say, 'But is this water poisoned?' It serves no purpose to stand and talk whilst you wait to perish. And so it is when I speak to people. What choice is there? You drink or you die!

I am like a blood transfusion to a bleeding world. There are those who will choose to accept my words. These will receive the blood transfusion. There are those of this world who will not accept. They will perish. Then there are those in certain countries who are not in a position to receive the blood transfusion. They do not have the choice. We must reach all peoples of this world, to at least enable them to have the choice. I have devoted the whole of my life to travelling the world with my message from spirit. I will talk to as many people as I possibly can, and then I will go home to where I came from. I will return to God's house. I am here for you. I would like to take you with me.

Hence the reason for writing this book which you hold in your hands. It is my hope that people may read this book long after I have departed this earth. If I can be heard by all people, my mission will be complete.

Chapter 7

Astral Travelling

We have long since established that we are all made up
of a physical body and a spiritual body, and that upon
death, our spiritual body leaves the physical to undergo
that exciting journey to a new home in a new world. The
two bodies, physical and spiritual, are joined by what is
known as the 'silver cord'. It is only our physical body
which needs rest and sleep. The spirit, of course, does
not, and so during sleep state, it can leave the body and
travel whilst still connected by the silver cord, which is
able to stretch infinitely. You may travel in this way,
either in this plane of existence or another. Distance is
no object. In the world of spirit, there is no time or
distance as we know them. This act of leaving the body,
or 'out of the body experiences', is called 'astral
travelling'.

Everyone astral travels, although it can be very difficult
for people with a material mind. Spiritually minded
people will astral travel far more frequently. However,
you may not be aware of this experience, as recall is
most unusual. If you were to remember all that you
experienced during astral travelling, it could make you
dissatisfied with your earthly life.

Whilst astral travelling, it is possible for you to travel
into another plane of existence, where you may speak to
friends or relatives who have long since passed through
that veil we call death.

Have you ever awakened with the memory of a dream in which you were perhaps talking with your grandmother who passed over many years ago? The truth is that you were, in fact, talking with her. You had been taken to visit her in the spirit world.

Perhaps you have experienced what is commonly known as 'déjà vu', where you visit a place for the first time, and yet it all seems so familiar. I have explained that this can be a product of reincarnation, but it can also be as a result of astral travelling on the earth plane.

It is possible for the spirit to leave the body, still joined by the silver cord, and travel anywhere in the world. Although you may not remember this experience, upon physically visiting that place you have a feeling that you have been there before.

In the same way, it is possible for you to be astral travelling whilst your friend, who lives perhaps in Australia, is doing the same. You can meet up and converse before returning to your physical bodies. Although you have no recollection of this, you may then wake up with this person on your mind, and so you telephone them, only to find that they were thinking of you too!

Similarly, people have been known to see the spirit of someone appearing before them, who is not, in fact, dead. This sounds incredible until you realise that this person is astral travelling, probably without realising, to visit their friend or relative.

Dreams are also as a result of astral travelling. I will go into more detail later, but suffice to say there are many experiences which astral travelling can bring.

Perhaps you have dreams at some time that you were falling, only to be awakened by a sudden jerk. This is caused by the spirit returning too rapidly to the body. This is a common experience, and whilst it can be rather startling, it is quite safe.

You may have had the sensation when just drifting off to sleep, when without apparent reason you are violently awakened by a sudden, powerful jerk. This is caused by too rapid a parting of the physical and the spirit bodies. It causes a contraction of the silver cord and the spirit body is snatched back into the physical vehicle.

During sleep state, I very often astral travel. I very often go home. As I remember my time in spirit, when I talk about going home, I am of course referring to going back to the high spirit realms, where I was before I was born into this earthly life.

Whilst I am astral travelling, I often visit various spirit planes and speak with many different people. I have even travelled downwards to that dark grey sphere. I talk to them and sometimes try to reclaim those lost spirits who have left our world in a state of sin.

The horror and darkness of these places, you could perhaps not imagine. They are like a bottomless pits with some poor souls very low down in these pits, and some rather hovering towards the top. By preaching and talking to these people, and by trying to help them, my words act rather as if I am throwing a lifeline to people who have fallen overboard and are drowning. Those who can realise how sinful a life they have led, and those who are truly sorry for their actions and wish to repent, can catch hold of this lifeline so that we may help them up.

There have been many reported cases of people who say that they died whilst on the operating table, or in similar circumstances. They say that they were lifted up, out of their bodies, and looked down upon themselves. This is yet another example of astral travelling. These instances are what are commonly called 'near death experiences'. The two bodies are, in fact, still connected by the silver cord, and so they were not, in truth, dead. Should the silver cord be broken, however, then death does take place, and there would then be no possible way of bringing the physical body back to life.

The body is to be looked upon as you would regard a suit of clothing. You wear it during the day, take it off at night, and eventually, when the suit has worn out, you discard it altogether.

The main thing to remember about astral travelling is that it is quite normal, safe and everyone does it. I find that those who can recall their experiences gained whilst astral travelling have no fear of death, and their lives and outlook upon life changes, to make them more spiritually minded. It is usually a most enjoyable experience.

Chapter 8

Dreams

Dreams are a phenomenon which have puzzled and intrigued man from the beginning of time. In order to define them, it must first be noted that they fall into several different categories.

Some dreams are products of your subconscious mind, some are symbolic messages or warnings from those in the spirit world, and some are as a result of astral travelling.

I spoke in the previous chapter of 'déjà vu', when it is caused by visiting a place where your spirit body has already been whilst you were in sleep state, but it is possible, not only to astral travel in this world, but to visit the spirit world whilst your body is sleeping.

People often tell me of dreams which involve themselves meeting and speaking to someone who has passed over to spirit. This can be that they have, in fact, met up with their loved one by astral travelling to the spirit world whilst in sleep state.

When your spirit body travels to the spirit world, those in spirit are able to communicate with you. They may give you information, knowledge, warnings or advice. This information is relayed along the silver cord to your brain, which receives it in picture form, rather like a television will receive pictures, and so your dreams are formed.

When spirit communicates in this manner, it is sometimes very direct, but usually these pictures or rather your dreams, are symbolic. That is to say that you must interpret your dreams in order to fully understand the meaning.

Recurring dreams can be quite common. If you have the same dream time and time again, this is because you have not identified what the dream means, and once you have done this, then you will not have the same dream again.

A fair proportion of my time is spent helping people to interpret their dreams, although the best person to do this is actually the person who has experienced it and for whom the message is intended. It is possible to learn to interpret your dreams by understanding what some of the signs or pictures mean, and relating them to your life. For example, if you were to dream that you were on a picnic, this could mean that you will shortly be enjoying an outing or get together with friends. A dream in which you are putting on new shoes could meant that you are being told to undertake a journey to visit someone, whilst a dream of fireworks may indicate that you are on the wrong pathway in life, and you must change direction in order to be successful.

It can be of tremendous help to you in your everyday life if you can learn to analyse and understand your dreams. Your friends and helpers in the spirit world are regularly giving you warnings. It is a pity if these warnings remain unheeded.

Although we do dream each and every night, we forget far more dreams than we remember. When our spirit body travels to the spirit world, we are capable of ingesting knowledge, like a sponge soaks up water. In order to return to our physical body, however, to our finite brain, the sponge must be squeezed, and much of what we took in is expelled. The tiny drops of spiritual knowledge which remain are very precious, and although we may not realise where we have gained them from, we should treasure rather than dismiss them.

Chapter 9

Communicating with Spirit

It is possible for anyone to communicate with spirit. Did you know that small babies see and hear those in the spirit world? Have you ever watched a baby looking up from his cot, smiling and making sounds into 'thin air'? They are seeing and listening to those in spirit. Of course, this is not so difficult to understand when you realise that babies have just entered this world from the world of spirit, and so of course they are very spiritual and very sensitive. However, as a child grows and develops in this physical, material world, it is easy to lose this ability of communicating with spirit. It is such a pity, and yet this is the case.

Perhaps you have a child who has so called 'imaginary' friends. Often, this is not imagination, but a spirit child who passed over very young, wishing to play with your child. This is quite harmless, and I would be inclined to encourage rather than discourage it. Too many people are told not to be silly, and that there is really no-one there, until they try to shut it out and being to believe that perhaps it is their imagination, or even that there is something wrong with them. Often, psychic awareness and ability is knocked out of children in this way.

In some parts of the world, mainly in what we may regard as uncivilised societies or primitive tribes, it is a normal, everyday ritual to continue communicating with those who have passed to spirit, just as the North

American Indians used to do. These so called primitive people are in many ways more spiritually advanced than those of us in so called 'civilised' societies. We could learn a lot from them.

Those in the spirit world very often talk to you. They are able to impress things upon your mind, putting ideas into your head. Just because you may not be able to hear their words spoken to you does not mean that they are not communicating with you. Listen to them, listen to that inner voice. You will find it easier in quiet meditation. Empty your mind of everything, keep your mind a blank, perhaps play tranquil music and allow those in spirit to impress upon you. With patience and practice, you will be amazed at the results.

Spirit can also communicate with you in your sleep state. You may wake up in the morning with the answer to your problem, or perhaps a feeling that you must telephone a friend, only to discover that they were hoping you would call, or perhaps in need of assistance. This is because spirit have told you so whilst you were asleep.

More sensitive people will find it easier to receive messages from spirit, and one important factor to bear in mind is that spiritually minded people will receive spiritual messages. Spirit are not able to send spiritual messages through a materially minded person.

Also, remember that communication is not just a one way channel. Talk to those in spirit, just as you would if they were here on the earth with you. You can also focus your mind upon those in spirit and direct your thoughts to them. They will be picked up and they will talk back to you.

Those on higher spiritual planes find it much easier to communicate with those on the earth plane than those on the lower planes do. Do not make the mistake of thinking that because they are on higher spiritual planes, they are further away. This is quite wrong. In spirit, there is no such thing as time and distance as we know it on the earth plane. There are just different dimensions. It usually follows that those who have been in spirit longer, find it easier to communicate than those who have only recently passed over. This is a general rule however, because someone who has led a very spiritual life on earth will go directly to one of the higher spirit planes, and they will find it a lot easier to communicate.

There are helpers in spirit who are trying to guide you, and remember that your loved ones who have passed on ahead of you like to keep in touch, just as they would do if they had gone away on holiday, or perhaps emigrated. You have nothing to fear from them. They are still the same people that you knew on earth, although they may have a greater understanding now if they are learning well. The reason they communicate is to help you, and in turn you can help so many other people by gaining spiritual knowledge and sharing that knowledge with others.

Those who have been demoted to the dark grey realms will usually not be able to communicate with those on the earth at all. But as it is that many people living on the earth plane try all sorts of ways to communicate with those in spirit, perhaps by using Ouija boards and the like, so those in the dark grey pit may try to communicate with those on the earth plane, and so it is that using the Ouija board is very, very wrong. It can, in fact, be downright dangerous, because by doing this, you can form a link with those in the dark grey pit, and there are some very evil people down there! I have been called in to help too many people who have dabbled with the Ouija board and have thus invited rather nasty characters who, having found a channel will not leave them alone. My advice to anyone who contemplates using the Ouija board is leave it alone. You do not realise what you might be tapping into.

Incidentally, the word 'Ouija board' comes from the German word 'Ja' and the French word 'Oui', both meaning yes. So you could call it a 'Yes Yes' board. It simply means putting the upturned glass on the table with a series of letters of the alphabet around the table, with Yes on one side and No on the other. Then people put their finger on the glass, ask, 'Is there anybody there?', and wait for it to move. This is the Ouija board.

I understand that a well-known games manufacturer brought out a game to play which is based on the Ouija board. This so called 'game' can be very dangerous, especially to young people who can be very vulnerable, and it should be banned. The people who brought this onto the market should be thoroughly ashamed of themselves.

Please forget any idea of using such a board, or any other such device. To the average person, this could be quite dangerous. People upon passing to spirit are the same people, and just as there are nice people in this world, so too there are evil people, and they too must pass over. They can cause much harm through the amateur using such devices as the Ouija board, and in any case, there is no need for them. You can learn to communicate far better without them.

Chapter 10

Psychic Development

From an early age, it was clear to everyone around me, especially my parents, that I was different from other children. For as long as I can remember, I have seen, heard or felt things that most other people do not. Yes, I am 'psychic', but all that means is that I am extra sensitive and perceptive to spiritual influences. I am categorised as a 'medium', that is to say that those in the spirit world who have passed on before us communicate with me.

Please note that I said they communicate with me. I cannot 'call anyone up'! People often ask me such things as, 'Can you contact my grandfather for me?' This is not possible. I simply tell people who in spirit is with them, and what, if anything, they have to say.

I possess a range of psychic gifts, which include clairvoyance, clairaudience, healing, trance-mediumship and transfiguration. Allow me to explain.

Clairvoyance is the psychic gift of seeing beyond normal sight. If I see someone in the spirit world, I can describe this person in detail using the gift of clairvoyance. The word is derived from the French words 'Claire' meaning clear, and 'Voir' which means to see. The literal meaning therefore is clear seeing. There are, in practice, two forms of clairvoyance, these being 'subjective', that is to say one receives a picture in the head, or mind's eye, and 'objective', where one sees with the open eye.

Clairaudience is the psychic gift of hearing. When those in the spirit world speak to me, I am using clairaudience. I usually either see or hear from those in the spirit world, but not necessarily both simultaneously. Different mediums have different gifts or combinations of gifts. Some may only see spirit, some only hear and so on. Like clairvoyance, clairaudience can also be subjective or objective, that is to say that a voice may be heard either 'in the head' or with the ears. Some mediums are only clairsentinent, that is to say they neither see nor hear from the spirit world, but they simply 'sense'.

Trance-mediumship is a very in-depth subject which I will touch upon in order to explain it as simply as I am able. It occurs when my spirit leaves my physical body, in much the same way as astral travelling, and is held in a hypnotic like state, while someone in spirit uses my body in order to communicate directly with others present. The amount of control this person may have over my body is variable. Some may only be able to speak, while others may also have full and accurate control of all my limbs. This is achieved with the use of psychic energy. In the case of transfiguration, the energy is used, rather than to control my limbs and vocal cords, to build up the facial features of someone in the spirit world, which overshadows my own. This is, of course, for recognition purposes, so that you may visually identify who in spirit is wishing to communicate.

The gift of spiritual healing must not be confused with faith healing as faith is not necessary. I have devoted a later chapter to this subject, but suffice at this point to say that it occurs when the healing power, which comes from God and is passed down through the spirit world, flows through the hands of the healer to correct the imbalance and therefore cure the patient. This can be done whilst the healer is conscious or, as is most usual in my case, in trance state. The doctor in spirit who helps me in the work enters my body and uses exceptional control in order to administer the healing. This form of spiritual healing is called contact healing, because the healer is in direct contact with the patient. 'Absent healing' occurs when a patient of mine is many miles away, but the healing power is directed to them by the power of thought.

One or more of the psychic gifts I have described are dormant in everyone. With professional guidance and a true desire to help others, each of you could develop your own psychic awareness.

The correct and safe way to do this is to join a psychic development circle, which is run by a competent and experienced medium who is able to take control of events and recognise any danger signs. The 'circle' is often referred to as a 'séance', although this word does tend to frighten people. In fact, all the word means is 'sitting'. It is the sitting together of a group of people who wish to conduct a psychic experiment. No-one should ever try sitting alone to develop, as this could be quite dangerous, and is certainly unwise.

Before one undertakes such a commitment however, one must be dedicated and certainly very patient, as psychic development cannot be rushed, and could take many, many years of regular sitting. In point of fact, no-one ever stops developing, but the rewards in being able to bring help and comfort to other people are well worth the wait.

Circles held in the evening often obtain the best results, although theoretically there is no reason why they should not be held at any time of day. In practice however, the evening seems to bring an atmosphere which is much more favourable to success. There seems to be a certain stillness and tranquillity which is absent during the day. Low lighting helps the atmosphere and is an aid to relaxation and concentration. Soft music may be played if desired. Ideally, one should 'sit' on a regular basis, perhaps one evening each week, and in my experience the best number of people to form a circle is eight. The best results are gained by regular sitting, and when all participants are on the same 'wavelength', or thinking along similar lines and with similar goals. Attitude of mind is all important. There must be 'harmony' within the circle if it is to achieve the optimum success. All minds may be focussed onto similar guidelines by preceding the circle with a spiritual discussion or a prayer. I always open and close each of my circles with a prayer, giving thanks, offering service and asking for protection. In a properly run circle, there is absolutely nothing whatsoever to fear.

The first thing that one must learn upon joining a development circle is to completely relax. This is of the utmost importance if spirit are to communicate. Deep, slow breathing and closed eyes can help, although you may, of course, keep your eyes open if you wish. In time, you will reach a stage of relaxation and spiritual frame of mind whereupon you are able to sit and allow spirit to communicate. You may experience objective or subjective clairvoyance or clairaudience, that is to say you may see or hear spirit. Perhaps to begin with you will experience odd and sudden temperature changes, or perhaps feel someone touching your face. Someone in the spirit world may even make an attempt to take you into trance. This can stimulate parts of the brain which have remained dormant, and may 'open the door' to greater psychic awareness.

Psychometry may also be developed in circle. I do not look upon it so much as a psychic gift, but rather as an 'art', which may be learned with practice, by anyone. The word is derived from the Greek, and its literal meaning is 'measurement of the soul' (that is to say, its intuitive capabilities), but I prefer to say that it is the art of 'reading' the character, surroundings and influences of an article, or a person, by the means of touch. You may learn to hold an article, for example a ring or watch, and by doing so learn much about the owner or perhaps the objects' usual surroundings. The impressions received may vary in intensity, and you must clear your mind in order to be successful. Have you ever shaken hands with a person and felt an instant like or dislike of them? This too is a form of psychometry.

True psychic development is nothing whatsoever to do with fortune telling. A genuine medium is an instrument to pass on messages from spirit to the recipient here on earth. This may include advice, words of comfort, or simply proof that life has real meaning, purpose and is eternal. I have never understood why some 'psychics' feel the need for crystal balls, tarot cards, tea leaves, palms, bumps on the head and other such paraphernalia. If you are truly psychic then you do not need to use such props, and if you are not, then you should not be doing psychic readings. It is a responsibility which should not be taken lightly.

I believe that everyone is born psychic to a degree, and it is possible for anyone to enhance their own psychic awareness, although not everyone is capable of becoming a fully-fledged practising medium. Most people, at some time in their life have a psychic experience. Psychic abilities and experiences have been suppressed for too long. People are afraid of ridicule and so keep their experiences secret. So often they come to me saying, 'I can tell you, because I know you will understand.' Throughout the ages, mediums have been worshipped, then burnt as witches, classed as geniuses, then lunatics. People are reluctant to believe what cannot be measured in earthly terms. Small wonder that people are afraid to speak out. It is not an easy pathway to travel, but as I said before, it is most rewarding.

There is a difference between psychic development and spiritual progression, although the two should go hand in hand. It is possible to be very spiritual, yet not have developed your psychic ability. It is equally possible, although not as favourable, to have well developed psychic ability yet not be very spiritual at all. To be a practicing medium who is able to help people to the full, both qualities are required.

As you develop your own psychic awareness, you should also adopt high spiritual values in everyday life. Never be selfish and always be prepared to give of yourself. Be natural and don't set yourself apart from others. There is only one reason why you should wish to develop, and that is to enable you to be of service to other people. You must have the desire to learn and understand, and most of all be sincere in your wish to help all people.

Mediumship is a heavy responsibility and it should always be treated as such, whether professional or otherwise. It is a sacred profession and psychic ability is a most sacred God given gift which should always be used for the good of others. Remember, we are all personally responsible and accountable for everything we do. Once we have opened ourselves up to this most powerful force, we must treat it always with the utmost respect.

Chapter 11

The Aura

Everyone has what is known as an 'aura' around them. This has been described as a magnetic-like field which surrounds the body, and it rather puts me in mind of the little boy on the breakfast cereal advertisement who has a glow of light around him.

Although vegetation has no spirit, all living things, including trees, plants, flowers and of course animals, have an aura. It is the life force of all things, and upon physical death, your aura will fade from the corpse and go with you to the spirit world. Hence a dead body has no aura. In a similar way, flowers growing in the field are surrounded by this glowing force, but when they are picked and placed in a vase, the aura gradually fades until the flowers are dead and there is no aura present at all.

The aura is what I call the clothing of the spirit. All of my life, I have seen the aura around people. It is seen as a cloud of coloured light which completely surrounds every part of the body.

There are many layers to the aura, rather as one would see upon slicing an onion in half, and it appears to stretch outwards from the body for around two to three feet. I see the part of the aura which is nearest to the body most clearly, as the clarity diminishes towards the edge. It appears as rays of coloured light, rather like a rainbow.

Throughout your earthly life, everything that you do, say, or even think is recorded in your aura. As I said, it is the clothing of the spirit, and when you pass over to the spirit world, carrying your aura with you, everyone sees you for exactly the person you are. There can be no pretending and no hiding. Everything is registered in your aura for all to see.

The study of a person's aura can reveal much information about them. By close observation, I can learn about their personality, emotions, the conditions around them and any health problems which they may have. It must be said that everyone's aura is constantly changing, as the feelings, moods and conditions around them are constantly changing.

I observe this information in two forms. I see pictures and signs within the aura which are symbolic, and which I must interpret to reveal much about events and conditions surrounding the person concerned, but I also gain much information by looking carefully at the many different colours and shades of colour which the aura contains. Each one has a different and unique meaning.

It would be impractical for me to list all of the innumerable colours, but I will give a short illustration of the strongest and most common of them. The meaning of these colours may also have a secondary interest to you. Are you aware that the colours you wear can affect how you feel? That the colours with which you have decorated your rooms can affect your mood and the colour of your own car can have an effect upon the way you drive? Knowing what each colour represents can help you. For example, if a lady is going to an interview for a job, I would not recommend that she wears a pink or pale blue suit, a navy blue one would be more acceptable. Why is that? Why do I say that people who have deep red cars tend to be more determined or aggressive drivers? Here is an outline of what the different colours and shade of colour represent. Apart from reading the aura, it can also help you in your everyday life.

RED – is a very strong colour, and an easy one to see. A clear, bright red shows strong determination and a lot of energy, whereas a rosy red can be affection or love. A pale, pinky red depicts nervousness or unstable character, and a very dark red can be either passion and sensuality or bad temper and aggression.

ORANGE – Orange is a nice, favourable colour to see in someone's aura. An abundance of orange shows consideration for others and unselfishness. Such people are mild-mannered, calm, not easily ruffled and are usually great thinkers. They are quiet people with much self-control.

YELLOW – A pleasant, golden yellow is a very spiritual colour. This shows a person who is on their correct pathway in life. A person with bright yellow like the sun within their aura can be completely trusted whereas a pure lemon yellow indicates great intellect. On the other hand, a dull yellow, like stale cheddar cheese, is a cowardly colour which identifies a person who is not to be trusted. A brownish yellow shows impure thoughts and low spirituality.

GREEN – A light, leaf green is a healing colour. Spiritual healers have a good percentage of this colour within their aura. This colour also shows a friendly type of person who is compassionate, caring and has a considerate nature. However, a person with a dark yellowish green is untrustworthy. This colour is often seen with confidence tricksters and the like. A dark, dull green reveals jealousy in a person.

BLUE – The problem with blue is that there are so many different shades of it. The shade of blue which resembles the sky on a warm summer's day is an extremely spiritual colour, showing a person with real spiritual knowledge and understanding, one who is not too interested in material wealth and possessions. A very pale blue shows a person who needs pushing to do anything, whereas a very dark or navy blue shows someone doing a worthwhile job, or who has a 'calling', perhaps a missionary or a nurse.

GREY – This colour represents negative aspects, a pessimistic nature perhaps. Grey around the head usually shows depression. A grey cloud around a person shows much confusion, that is to say someone who is 'lost' or mixed up. Grey patches can also pinpoint medical problems.

Of course, here I have only touched upon what some of the colours mean in an attempt to give you some understanding. By developing your own psychic awareness, you too may develop the ability to see the aura. It must always be remembered of course that the colours of the aura are constantly changing, depending on the person's moods, thoughts, actions, ideas, emotions and medical conditions.

Incidentally, dogs as well as other animals are able to see the aura around people. This is why dogs are often able to judge a person's character. They are very sensitive to psychic experiences.

Although one is rarely able to see and read their own aura, you can in fact feel it on occasions. Try this experiment. Hold your hands out in front of you about two feet apart and with the palms facing together. Slowly bring your hands together. You will discover that when your hands are still inches apart, you can 'feel' the force. The closer your hands get, the stronger the force, and when your palms are only about an inch apart, you should be able to clearly feel this, almost like placing the identical poles of two magnets together.

As a child in the school playground, did you ever play the game where you face the wall whilst a group of children silently creep towards you from behind? You must turn in time to catch them moving. You can actually feel when someone is close to you without seeing or hearing them at all. You will experience this in everyday life. You will instinctively know when someone is standing behind you as your aura touches theirs. There are many ways in which you can experience the coming together of two people's auras.

Chapter 12

Spirit Guides and Helpers

Throughout your earthly life, you each have with you a spirit guide and spirit helpers. You have one spirit guide who is with you from the day you are born until the day you pass over to spirit yourself. A spirit guide has been in spirit for many years, perhaps hundreds of years our time. I say 'our time' because as I have said, there is no such thing as time as we know it in the spirit world.

A guide must be spiritually advanced, with great knowledge, and they must have progressed to one of the high spirit planes. These highly spiritual people from the realms of spirit voluntarily give up further advancement to spend an earthly lifetime with you. They wish to help you and it is their job to try to guide you along life's pathway. They may impress upon your mind and encourage you, although, because God gives everyone free will, they cannot make you do anything you do not wish to do.

When you pass over to spirit, your guide will be with you, helping you to make that transition, and they will remain with you whilst the whole of your life is analysed. Also, during your life on earth, you will have any number of spirit helpers near you, helping you along the way. Some may only stay for a short while, and others may stay longer as you pass through various stages of life. Each will bring their own expertise and knowledge to assist you. Each is there for a particular reason. These helpers are usually quite highly developed spiritually, and it is true to say that by helping you, they too are learning and advancing.

Like attracts like. By this, I mean that you may have a particular helper or helpers who are knowledgeable in your particular field. For instance, if you are a writer, you may be assisted by someone who was a writer themselves whilst here on earth. If you are a nurse or a doctor, you may have with you someone who used to work in the medical profession.

Have you ever looked at a painting and said 'The artist must have been inspired'? In fact, that could be very true. The artist may well have received spiritual inspiration. If you chose to allow it, you too can be inspired by your helpers in spirit.

It is approximately three hundred years since my own guide passed to spirit at the end of his last incarnation, and we are still good friends. I have seen and heard him since I was a child, but just because you may not be able to see or hear your own guide, do not think he is not there helping and influencing your mind in the hope that you take his advice. Although you should listen to the advice of your guide, you must also remember the importance of personal responsibility. That is to say that you will be held personally responsible for all your actions, therefore you alone must decide what actions to take. You must always do what you feel is right for you.

I also have a number of doctors in spirit who assist in the healing work. They have gained not only medical knowledge whilst here on earth, but now also spiritual knowledge since their passing and so they are ideal for helping to administer the spiritual healing.

Remember that your own spirit helpers are there for a purpose. They will assist you all they can if you will only allow them to. They cannot, however, help you to win the pools or pick a horse in a race. That is not what they are there for. They are there to help you spiritually.

You may talk to your spirit guide or helpers, and you may send your thoughts out to them, but you do not pray to them. You must pray only to God, and your helpers in spirit will inspire you always to do God's will, as it is always important to remember that it is His will that must be done, not ours.

Life on earth is not meant to be easy, but we can take comfort in the fact that throughout our earthly lives we are never alone. We have those in spirit helping us, especially our own spirit guide and spirit helpers. Your spirit guide is there for the sole purpose of helping you. He is your own personal guide; there to guide, guard, protect and advise you, and only you. Even though he is with you, he can also travel in the spirit world, but is never far away.

If you were to need his help when he was elsewhere, he would return to you in an instant. Rather like the deep sea diver pulls on the rope to indicate that he needs help and wishes to be pulled up, your thoughts act as if you are pulling on an imaginary rope which extends between yourself and your guide. He can pick up on your thoughts and be there in a second. We are never alone. It is comforting, is it not, when you come to realise that help is only a thought away.

Chapter 13

Spiritual Healing

Spiritual healing is a most sacred and divine gift. It is certainly not something new. Healing is as old as the world itself.

The healing power comes from God. It comes from Him and is channelled through those in the high spirit realms, through the doctors in spirit and is administered through the healer's hands, to the patient. I am often told that patients feel a heat or vibration from my hands although I do not feel this myself. As you see, the spiritual healer is simply an instrument, a link in a chain, and we must never forget that the healing power comes from God.

Spiritual healing is not to be confused with faith healing. Faith healing implies that faith is needed in the healing process, but this is not the case with spiritual healing. It does not rely on faith. Healing has been successful in small babies, and even in animals who, of course, do not have faith. On the contrary, spiritual healing is a very real power.

I always say that there is no such thing as an incurable illness or disease, only illnesses which the medical profession has not yet found a cure for. There is not an illness known that spiritual healing cannot help with. Although I am not saying that it is always one hundred per cent successful. I have found that it is beneficial to most people. The very least we hope for is that the patient receives some relief, and at best they are completely cured.

I have been using my healing gift for many years, and I now have several healing centres throughout Britain. As I have said, I am helped in my healing work by doctors in the spirit world. Whilst conducting healing, I often work in what is known as a trance state, that is to say that I allow a spirit doctor to control my body to perform the healing. The spirit doctors have gained not only medical knowledge whilst they were on the earth, but also spiritual knowledge since their passing, to enable them to continue their mission of healing the sick.

From the age of sixteen, I have worked with many spirit doctors. The team which work with me now is headed by Dr Albert Schweitzer, who won the Nobel Peace Prize in 1952 and passed to spirit as recently as 1965.

During Albert's earthly life he achieved much and is probably most famous for his work with the lepers in Africa. He was regarded by many as brilliant and saintly, and yet now, having passed to spirit, he says that he could have done so much more, and that when all is put in perspective, he understood very little. His work was his life and he wishes to continue now his mission of helping the sick.

Anyone who receives spiritual healing should not disregard the medical profession. This would be foolish. Healers should work more closely with doctors, not be their rivals. I am fortunate in that I have been allowed, and on occasion indeed invited, to work in hospitals administering healing. Although some doctors may frown upon the idea, others are becoming more open-minded towards spiritual healing. After all, we are all working with the best interest of the patient in mind.

Spiritual healing has been proven time and time again. It is not God's will that anyone be ill. It is unnatural, that is to say it is against nature, or contrary to God's natural laws. Where there is illness, there is an imbalance, and it is the healer's objective to correct this imbalance.

The job of the healer is simplicity itself. He is, as I have said, just a link in the chain, a channel through which the healing power is administered. It is not necessary for the healer to have any medical knowledge whatsoever. Indeed, I have none at all and yet people have come to me with all kinds of ailments from leukaemia to a bad back and have been cured.

Many people ask, 'Can healing help with this illness?' or, 'Can healing help with that problem?' My answer is always the same, 'Come along and receive spiritual healing. It certainly cannot make you any worse. At the very least, you will receive some comfort, and at best a complete and long lasting cure.'

Chapter 14

Absent Healing

I receive hundreds of letters from people throughout the world who are in need of spiritual healing, and of course it is simply not possible for me to see everyone personally. However remarkable results can be achieved by way of absent healing.

This occurs when, with the very real power of thought, I am able to direct the divine healing power to a patient who is not able to receive spiritual healing by means of contact.

The doctors in spirit are able to travel in an instant, again using the power of thought, to wherever in the world the patient may be, and the healing may be administered in this way.

I can direct the healing power to anyone, anywhere. In the final pages of this book, you will find an email address which you may write to, should you require my services. Please include in your email your name and the nature of your problem.

If you are in need of healing, then you must help me to help you. I administer spiritual healing to everyone who requests it. I direct the healing power at 10.00pm our time (22.00hrs) each evening, by means of the doctors in the spirit world.

If you are in receipt of absent healing, it helps enormously if at around this time, you can follow this short procedure, which should last a minimum of ten minutes.

You must be seated or lying, and be completely relaxed. It may help to play slow, relaxing, instrumental music if you wish. Take a couple of deep breaths. Now, imagine the aura around you. This is a cloud of light, completely surrounding every inch of your body, containing many colours, like a rainbow. Think of the colour green, a nice leaf green. This colour is becoming more predominant and surrounding your body, around your feet, up your legs, up your body, around your neck and shoulders, and finally your head. This will make you feel good, relaxed and happy. The healing power is getting ready to work.

Now concentrate especially on your problem areas, so that the power can be directed there, taking away any pain or discomfort. The healing power is absorbed into your body. Picture the green fading away, leaving the aura looking a bright, silvery blue colour, shining, radiating.

As you continue to sit there, relaxed and feeling good, your whole body is enveloped in spiritual warmth. It is nice to say a prayer of thanksgiving at this time.

Do please let me know what you may experience, as well as the results. People have, in the past, reported all kinds of strange experiences during the healing. Some feel very little, whilst others experience things such as seeming to be encapsulated in a bubble, feeling hands upon the problem area, feeling heat or vibration, seeing an image of my face or even the doctor in spirit who is with me. Do not fear anything which you may experience at this time. You are quite safe.

I am convinced that together, we can administer the divine healing power that comes from God, to enable you to become well.

Chapter 15

A Message From The High Spirit Realms

During the writing of this book, a spirit teacher who has over many centuries progressed to the high spirit realms impressed upon me the desire to convey his own personal message to the readers of this book. I have decided to pass this message to you exactly as he passed it to me. Word for word. The message went as follows:

'Good day, my friends. I bring you blessings from spirit. Just because you may not see your friends and helpers from the worlds of spirit around you, does not mean that they are not there, and very close, wishing to help you, guide you, direct you and comfort you.

It may well be difficult for you to accept the reality of invisible worlds completely surrounding your physical, material world. You are, of course, aware of the visible nature around you, but you can also be aware of the invisible.

Death does not turn a sinner into a saint, or a fool into a wise man. The mentality is the same as before. You are exactly the same person after passing through that veil called death. You will take with you your desires, false teachings and religious or agnostic beliefs. That is why spiritual knowledge is so important.

We see all too many people passing from the earth plane, who are so confused, lost, mixed up and haunted by fear because of their pre-conceived ideas. We wish to help you people, to teach you real spiritual truths, but you must open your minds to receive these teachings. Be guided by us.

There are people in your world who are selfish, misguided or have evil inclinations. Many of these people, upon their passing, carry these inclinations with them. Many will be lost in the darkness until they can see the errors of their ways and be helped, but many seek an outlet for their tendencies, until such time as their destructive desires are outgrown. Lacking physical bodies to carry out their deeds, many are attracted to the magnetic light which emanates from you people on the earth plane, and consciously or unconsciously, they attach themselves to these magnetic auras, enabling them to influence the minds of you people. These earthbound spirits are what some have termed as devils, or unclean spirits throughout the ages.

Prayer, purity of thought and spiritual knowledge offer protection from such influences. Possessing spirits are frequently mentioned throughout the bible. The belief in spirit possession was common during the time of the apostles. They were given the ability to cast out evil spirits, just as Jesus used to do.

Now, we say unto you, watch your every word, deed and thought. Purity of these three will enable you to be surrounded by angels, and evil entities cannot draw close. But an impure mind, or careless thought, or selfish deed, can allow those of lower intelligence to draw close.

Allow us to give you spiritual knowledge that may rain down upon you, acting as a spiritual shower to refresh you. Gain as much spiritual knowledge as you can during your earthly life. Be clean of mind and spirit, so that when you pass over to spirit, you can be with us on the high spirit realms. God be with you.'

Chapter 16

Jesus and The Christ Spirit

As I have explained, every one of us is made up of an earthly body and a spirit. When the physical body dies, the spirit, of course, lives on. We were all spirit before our physical birth, we are spirit now and we will always be, and so it is with the Christ Spirit.

What did Jesus mean when he said, 'Abraham rejoiced that he was to see the time of my coming. He saw it and was glad'? This has to be a reference to life being eternal, as Abraham 'died' many years before Jesus was born.

What did Jesus mean when he said, ' Before Abraham was born I am'? The Christ Spirit has always been since the very beginning. This is outlined in the first chapter of John in the New Testament

Two thousand years ago, the Christ Spirit decided to have a physical life on earth, to live amongst the people in order to spread a very important message and to heal the sick. He was born to Joseph and Mary, and they called him Jesus. Jesus lived a physical life on earth for just thirty three years, and then he died.

Of course, only the physical body dies, not the spirit, and the spirit of Jesus the 'Christ Spirit', returned to where he had come from. In John chapter 16, verse 28, Jesus says, 'I did come from the Father and I came into the world, and now I am leaving the world and going to the Father.' This clearly indicates that when he departed this world of ours, he was returning to where he had originally come from. You see, as I explained earlier, we all have a number of lives on earth. The Christ Spirit has had a number of lives on earth. He was called 'Jesus' in one of those lives.

'Christians' make many fundamental mistakes, and the most common of these is to say 'Jesus Christ'. This is quite misleading. Jesus was a man born in Bethlehem two thousand years ago. The Christ Spirit, however, (a part of God) has always been since the very beginning of time. Allow me to explain.

I explained when referring to 'your higher self', that upon reaching the high spirit planes you will become, not one singular person, but an accumulation of all your past lives, with all the knowledge which you acquired in them. In the case of Jesus, what happened was that he was born to the earth as we all are, and then at the age of thirty, whilst still here on the earth, he became the accumulation of his past existences on earth and in spirit. He gained all the knowledge he required to do the job he was here to do. He then left his home and family, and began his mission.

The Christ Spirit has always been, is now, and will always be. He chose to live a physical, human life on earth to teach people and to act as a signpost, pointing the way. Spirit cannot have an earthly life, living and speaking to the human race, without a vehicle in which to do so. (The vehicle being a physical body). The sole reason for Jesus having a life on earth was so that the Christ Spirit might speak to this world. It is a pity that his teachings have, to a large extent, been misinterpreted, manipulated or misunderstood over the years, when really his message is so simple. I believe his greatest teaching to be The Sermon on The Mount. Please read it carefully, for those who read it, understand it and live by it, have nothing to fear. They are very spiritual.

The sermon acts as a little map, showing the way from here on earth to heaven. Some people would have you believe that when you die, you go directly to heaven. What gives you the right to go to heaven just because you die? Everyone dies, and everyone lives on after death, but not everyone will go to heaven, because they do not know the way. They are lost.

The Christ Spirit, during his earthly life as Jesus, gave us the way. No-one can use the excuse that they did not know.

Some people seem to be under the impression the physical body of Jesus lived on after death, and in fact that his physical body is still living on. Of course, physical bodies do not live on, only the spirit lives on, and it is the Christ Spirit that lives on now, and always will.

Simply believing in Jesus is not enough to carry you to heaven. One must live a spiritual life and follow the 'map' he gave, and then you may begin to climb that steep stairway to heaven.

Some Christians would have you believe that because Jesus died on the cross, he carries all our sins. They are saying that no matter how sinful you are in this life, whether you are a murderer, a rapist or a thief, providing you turn and accept Christ before your time is up, then they say you will be saved. Your sins will be forgiven you! I tell you this; we are all personally responsible for all our thoughts, words and actions. We cannot use Christ as a scapegoat. The Christian Church says that Jesus died for us, but I tell you this – JESUS LIVED FOR US!

Jesus stood as a great friend of the poor, and he was a great healer, he comforted those in sorrow, and above all, the whole of his preaching reflects his love of our Eternal Father, God.

He foretold the happiness that can await you in the spirit world, and he told how to live our lives on earth, so that we can learn the lessons we were sent here to learn. He devoted his life to teaching people about life, both life on earth and the life to come, and he certainly proved that life is eternal.

First and foremost, Jesus was a reformer, and he was made to suffer for his beliefs. Let us put a few facts correct concerning the life of Jesus. Firstly, let us talk about the mystery which seems to surround the birth of Jesus. I will tell you what actually happened.

Mary and Joseph, the parents of Jesus, were put into a trance-like state whereupon, filled with the Holy Spirit, Joseph made love to Mary. As neither one had any recollection of this afterwards, there is little wonder that they could not understand how Mary had become pregnant. However, pregnant she was, and it says in the bible that someone appeared to Joseph in a dream, and said that he should take Mary as his wife, which is what he did.

The story concerning their journey to Bethlehem, where Joseph had to register, is very true. It is also true that there was no room at the inns. Jesus was born in a cave where livestock was kept, and the famous wise men were actually astrologers. (See Matthew 2. 'Soon afterwards, some men who studied the stars came from the East to Jerusalem!')

Jesus returned with his parents to live in Nazareth, where he grew up and had his childhood. Joseph, his earthly father, was a general builder. They were quite a wealthy family, which is quite credible when you consider that the 'wise men' had left them gold. Jesus learned the family trade.

At the age of thirty, Jesus became the 'accumulation', with the knowledge and wisdom which belongs to the Christ Spirit. He walked away from his home, brothers, sisters and parents (Jesus being the eldest of quite a large family) and left everything behind. He knew it was time for his mission to begin. He had a very important message to spread.

Jesus went around the country spreading his word, teaching the people and conducting healing. He was thrown out of the churches because they didn't like to hear the truth. They felt comfortable in the teachings that they were spreading. They could do without anyone 'rocking the boat'.

He chose to teach and preach wherever he could. On the hillside, at the waterside, on the mountain, and in people's houses, including the houses of sinners! When people said, 'Why is it, if you are a holy man, that you are mixing with these people, these tax collectors and sinners?' Jesus replied, 'It is not the healthy that need a doctor, but the sick!' What, of course, he was saying is what is the point of preaching to the converted? He was prepared to preach wherever anyone would listen...

His mission lasted for some three years. The orthodox religious leaders of the day were out to stop him. Eventually, they succeeded, and Jesus was crucified. This was the end of Jesus' earthly life.

Three days later, Mary, Jesus's mother and Mary Magdalene, who had known Jesus well for some time, went to where the body had been buried. Then, according to the gospel John 20 verse 14, 'Then Mary turned round and saw Jesus standing there, but she didn't know that it was Jesus. 'Woman, why are you crying?' Jesus asked her, 'Who is it that you are looking for?' She thought he was the gardener. Why didn't Mary, who had followed Jesus for so long, recognise her Master? In the gospel according to Luke 24.13, 'On that same day, two of Jesus's followers were going to a village about eleven kilometres from Jerusalem, and they were talking to each other about all the things that happened. As they talked and discussed, Jesus himself drew near and walked along with them. They saw him but did not recognise him.

Why did they not recognise him? These people had spent the last two or three years with him, living with him, sleeping with him, eating with him and working with him. Why did they not recognise him? Also, whilst a group of the disciples were behind locked doors, it is written that Jesus appeared to them. This means that he passed through solid walls. How can you account for all this? The answer is very simple. It was the 'Christ Spirit'who appeared to Mary. It was the Christ Spirit that was with the two disciples walking along the road. It was the Christ Spirit that appeared to the disciples behind locked doors. It is important to differentiate between Jesus and the Christ Spirit, then one can understand the bible teachings much more clearly.

Chapter 17

Christianity And The Bible

Many people say that I am very religious and yet there is not a religion in the world today that I agree with. They say that I am a Christian, yet there is not a Christian religion that I agree with. As for myself, I let others decide what to call me. I dislike labels, and after all, what is in a name?

Orthodox Christianity certainly does not hold all the answers. Christians believe in Jesus, and if only his words had been properly recorded at the time he walked Palestine, then perhaps the Christian Church would not be in the mess it is in today.

I view the bible rather like an overgrown garden. Remove all the weeds and you will see beautiful flowers. By this I mean, of course, that there is much nonsense in the bible, but also, I must emphasise, there is a lot of truth.

As I read the New Testament, the teachings of Jesus, I sometimes wonder if certain church leaders read the same bible as I do. There are, of course, many mistakes in the bible. People may not like me to say this, but much of what is taught in the Church today is, in fact, in direct conflict with the teachings of Jesus. This is, however, very true. Allow me to demonstrate.

In Matthew 6:5, 'When you pray, do not be like the hypocrites! They love to stand up and pray in the houses of worship and on the street corners, so that everyone will see them. I assure you, they have already been paid in full. But when you pray, go to your room, close the door and pray to your Father, who is unseen, and your Father, who sees what you do in private, will reward you.'

This quotation quite clearly is an instruction which the Christian Church today chooses to ignore. It acts in direct conflict to what Jesus taught.

Matthew 23:9, again Jesus speaking, 'And you must not call anyone here on earth 'Father', because you have only the one Father in heaven.' Do Catholics read this, or do they choose to ignore it when they call their priests 'Father'? Jesus quite clearly said, 'You must not call anyone 'Father'', so why do they?

Mark 12:38 Jesus said, 'Watch out for the religious leaders who like to walk around in their long robes and be greeted with respect, who choose the reserved seats in churches and the best places at feasts, and make a show of saying long prayers. Their punishment will be all the worse!'

Church leaders, you have been warned!

Matthew 23:34, Jesus speaking – 'And so I tell you that I will send you prophets and wise men and teachers. You will kill some of them, crucify others and whip others.'

Throughout history, spiritually gifted and inspired people have been sent to the earth, and continually they have been persecuted by the Church. They have been persecuted by the clergy who fear the loss of their own positions and livelihoods.

Luke 12:52 – Jesus talking to the church leaders. 'How terrible for you teachers of the law, you have kept the key that opens the door to the house of knowledge. You yourselves will not go in, and you stop those that are trying to get in.'

What Jesus is saying here to the so called experts of religion, is that they hide the truth from people. They cannot accept it for themselves, and so they prevent others from having the chance to accept it. Jesus says in Matthew 15 that the church leaders are the blind leading the blind. This is as true of our church leaders today as it was two thousand years ago.

Many people make the mistake in thinking that Jesus was God, but Jesus never professed to be God. In fact, quite the opposite. On many occasions, he referred to his Father God who sent him. In John 6:38 he says, 'Because I have come down from heaven to do not my own will but the will of Him who sent me.' Clearly, Jesus is saying that he was in spirit before he was born, and clearly he is saying that he is not God, as he refers to 'God who sent him'.

Matthew 24:36 Jesus, speaking about the end of the world says that even he does not know when this will be.

Only God knows that. Again, a clear reference that Jesus is not God.

In Matthew 12:27, Jesus is accused of doing the work of the devil. Mediums are often accused of this also.

In Matthew 22:31, 'Now, as for the dead rising to life, haven't you ever read what God has told you? He said, 'I am the God of Abraham, the God of Isaac, and the God of Jacob.' He is the God of the living, not of the dead. When the crowds heard this, they were amazed at his teaching.'

Here, Jesus is clearly saying that Abraham, Isaac and Jacob are still alive in the spirit world, and if they are, so too are all the other people who have died. What better teachings are there that there is life after death and that we do not remain in the grave waiting for some day of judgement, but rather we are judged on the day that we 'die'.

Matthew 17:1 - 'Six days later, Jesus took with him Peter and the brothers James and John, and led them up a high mountain where they were alone. As they looked on, a change came over Jesus. His face was shining like the sun and his clothes were dazzling white. Then the three disciples saw Moses and Elijah talking with Jesus.'

Here, Jesus is seen talking with two people who had, of course, been dead for many years. Both Moses and Elijah are from the Old Testament. How can the Church condemn a medium who talks to those who have passed over many years before, when this was exactly what

Jesus did? Where it says that Jesus's face shone like the sun, this quite clearly was transfiguration.

Matthew 11:14 – Jesus speaking about John the Baptist. 'John is Elijah, whose coming was predicted.' If this is not a direct reference to reincarnation, I do not know what is! Jesus said, 'John is Elijah.' Now, Elijah is from the Old Testament, hundreds of years before, so quite clearly, Jesus is saying that John the Baptist was Elijah reincarnated.

Matthew 26:36 talks about Jesus going away to pray alone, leaving the three disciples on guard duty, but they fell asleep. Three times, Jesus went away to pray and three times, he came back only to find his disciples asleep. Who was able to record what Jesus said or did? If the disciples were asleep, who recorded what was said?

There are many such errors in the bible. Most of Jesus's teachings have been badly reported and distorted. Still more have been lost or disregarded.

In Luke 18:38 following Jesus preaching to the disciples and trying to teach them, it goes on to say, 'But the disciples did not understand any of these things. The meaning of the words was hidden from them, and they did not know what Jesus was talking about.'

Is it any wonder that the gospels appear at times to be so confusing and contradictory? The gospels were written by men who did not understand. They did not understand half of what Jesus said to them or tried to teach them. These gospels where then translated several times by other men with even less understanding. Bad translations were made, and so on. It is easy to see why the bible cannot be accepted totally on its face value. There can be none so blind as to declare that the bible is the complete and infallible word of God.

Some people will say that they believe the bible to be the word of God, and that it should be taken quite literally. To people who believe this, I have to say that I hope they do not eat shellfish, cut their hair or shave. I hope they do not wear cloths woven of more than one cloth, or summon their flock to church by bells, since all of these are strictly forbidden by the bible.

In John 5:58 Jesus said: 'The absolute truth is that I was in existence before Abraham was ever born.' Quite clearly, Jesus, filled with the Holy Spirit, is saying that the Christ Spirit has always been since the beginning of time.

Right in the very beginning of the bible, Genesis 1:26, it says, 'Then God said, 'And now we will make human beings, and they will be like us and resemble us.''

Who are these 'we' and 'us' that are mentioned? I will tell you this in all truth – they are God and the Christ Spirit, who have both been in existence since the beginning of time.

It would be very easy for me to go on and on about all the teachings of Jesus and how people have misunderstood them. Quite clearly, even Christian religions have got the message completely wrong.

People accept what they are told all too easily. Everyone should think for themselves and reach their own conclusions. Are you aware, for instance, that nowhere in the bible is it recorded that it was a stable in which Jesus was born? Did you know that nowhere does it say that three kings visited the child?

What it does say, in Matthew chapter 2, is that 'Some men who studied the stars' visited Jesus, but no mention of kings or how many there were. Matthew also speaks of 'The house where Jesus was born'.

We are told these stories and brainwashed from an early age, and we accept blindly. We should not follow like sheep, without question. We are each personally responsible for ourselves, and we should, after taking into account all angles, reach our own conclusions.

There are some points in the bible which are impossible to believe. No-one can honestly say that they believe every word of the bible. I will give you some examples of absurdity from the Old Testament.

I begin with the story of Adam and Eve. God says to Adam that he must not eat the fruit of the tree, because if he does, he will die the same day. Eve then encounters a talking snake! This snake tells her to eat the fruit and she will not die. So she eats the fruit and gives some to the man. They do not die. Does this mean that the snake was right and God was wrong?

In Genesis 3:8, Adam and Eve hid from God and he called out 'Where are you?' Is this the same God which Jesus speaks of? The God who know how many hairs are on your head, the God who knows everything, and yet he could not find them?

At the age of one hundred and thirty, the bible tells us that Adam had a son, Seth. Eight hundred years later, at the age of nine hundred and thirty, he died! Seth had a son, Enoch, when he was one hundred and five, and died at the age of nine hundred and twelve, and so on.

In Genesis 6:3, God decides to put his foot down. 'I will not allow people to live forever, they are mortal. From now on, they will live no longer than a hundred and twenty years.'

Then, when Noah was six hundred years old, the flood came! He built an ark which was a hundred and thirty three metres long, twenty two metres wide and thirteen metres high. Onto this, he was supposed to have two of every kind of animal in the world. Apart from the fact that the biggest tanker in the world today could not achieve this, how did get polar bears, which are only found on the North Pole, or kangaroos from Australia?

Thankfully, Noah's grandfather Methuselah was drowned in the flood at the tender age of nine hundred and sixty nine! Had it not been for the flood, he might have lived forever! Noah himself lived to be nine hundred and fifty!

In Genesis 19, Lot has sex with both of his daughters, who become pregnant and have children!

In Genesis 32, Jacob wrestles with God, and God pleads with Jacob to let him go!

In Exodus 4:24, God tries to kill Moses. Luckily, he fails!

How ridiculous! There are many, many such examples in the bible. Indeed, I could write another book filled with all the absurdities, but it must be remembered that there are many truths in the bible also. We must read, interpret and take care in cutting away the weeds, and then we may see the beautiful flowers.

God gave us very simple laws to follow. These are the ten commandments.......

- You must love God with all your heart.

- You must not worship any other God.

- You must not misuse the name of God.

- You must observe the Sabbath and keep it holy.

- You must respect your father and your mother.

- You must not commit murder.

- You must not commit adultery.

- You must not steal.

- You must not accuse anyone falsely.

- You must not desire what another person has.

These are God's commandments. Very simple laws to follow, and Jesus gave the people a new commandment. He said, 'You must love one another. As I have loved you, so you must love one another. If you have love for one another, then everyone will know that you are my disciples.' This seems a very simple instruction. But is it that simple? It can sometimes be very difficult to love other people, but it is perhaps the most important lesson that we can learn.

I was speaking to a gentleman who had been in spirit just a few short years of our time, and he was saying, 'When we pass over to spirit, of course we have much to learn, and the hardest lesson I have to learn is to love everyone,' 'There are, he continued, some people that I don't particularly like very much. How am I to love these people?' But I tell you this - this man will not progress in spirit any further until he has mastered this lesson. This is a lesson we must learn now whilst we are still on the earth plane, because if we can learn now to love one another, we will not then have this lesson to learn in spirit. The lessons we do learn now, we will not have to learn again, but lessons we do not learn now, we will have to learn when we pass to spirit.

It is when you are in spirit, and still having problems learning certain lessons, that it is put to you that you perhaps should be reincarnated. Perhaps you should have another life on the earth plane to try and see if you can learn the lessons there. The problem with most people living on the earth today is that they are too materialistic and not very spiritual. Material possessions are very, very important to people. A big bank balance, holidays abroad, they must buy a second car because the next door neighbour has two cars and so on. I tell you this, material possessions accumulated whilst on the earth plane, you cannot take with you. Spiritual knowledge that you have acquired on the earth plane, you can take with you, and so it is that we should be putting our emphasis more on the spiritual and less on the material.

When a Jewish leader asked Jesus what it was he must do to enter the kingdom of heaven, Jesus replied that he must keep God's commandments, but the Jewish leader said, 'Ever since I was young, I have obeyed all these commandments.' When Jesus heard this, he said to him, 'There is still one thing you need to do. Sell all you have and give the money to the poor, and you will have riches in heaven.' But when the man heard this, he became very sad, because he was very rich. Jesus saw that he was sad and said, 'How hard it is for rich people to enter the kingdom of God. It is much harder for a rich person to enter the kingdom of God, than for a camel to pass through the eye of a needle.' That teaching is as true today as it has always been. In other words, rich people have got no chance. It is impossible to be both materialistic and spiritual. Rich people have that lesson to learn. We have all of us seen the people going to church on a Sunday, the wealthy people, and the ladies in their best hats dripping in jewellery. These people are nothing but hypocrites. They have a very important lesson to learn. Would they even contemplate giving their money away to the poor? Sooner or later, they will have to learn this lesson. Better for them to learn it sooner, rather than later.

A church can be a nice place in which to feel at peace with God and pray alone. However, churches are widely misused. People go to church to ease their consciences or to look good and respectable in the eyes of their neighbours. They go inside, take part in the service and are 'Christians' for an hour. They then go home and forget about it until next Sunday.

They sing hymns, but do not think about the words they are singing. They recite the service and prayers in a parrot fashion and do not stop to consider or even understand what they are saying. Prayers are only acceptable if they come from the heart. Recited words do not fool God. When people recite the Lord's Prayer, do they know what it is they are saying? People do not stop to think what they are saying. The version which everyone recites is vastly out of date. People in the reign of King James may well have understood it, but we are now in the twenty first century. Perhaps it is time for the Lord's Prayer to be updated. I would say.....

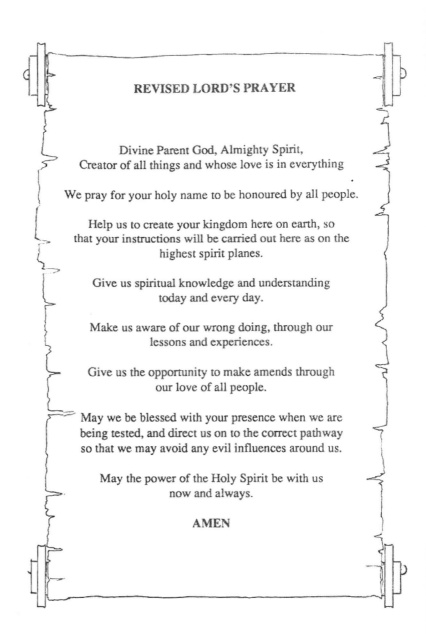

REVISED LORD'S PRAYER

Divine Parent God, Almighty Spirit,
Creator of all things and whose love is in everything

We pray for your holy name to be honoured by all people.

Help us to create your kingdom here on earth, so
that your instructions will be carried out here as on the
highest spirit planes.

Give us spiritual knowledge and understanding
today and every day.

Make us aware of our wrong doing, through our
lessons and experiences.

Give us the opportunity to make amends through
our love of all people.

May we be blessed with your presence when we are
being tested, and direct us on to the correct pathway
so that we may avoid any evil influences around us.

May the power of the Holy Spirit be with us
now and always.

AMEN

When you pray, be completely relaxed; be away from any outside interference. Prayer is a very real power. If your prayer is said in truth and in sincerity, it will be directed to the highest spirit planes. Some people will say that when they pray, their prayers are not answered. All prayers are answered, but of course, the answer sometimes has to be no. It very much depends, of course, on what it is you are asking for. Are you ready for what you are asking for?

If my daughter, aged five, was to ask me for a computer, then of course the answer would have to be no, as she is not yet ready for a computer. Your parents know best. And so it is when you ask your parent God. Sometimes the answer has to be no. Also, it is very true that God works in mysterious ways, His wonders to perform. We should use prayer wisely, and not bargain with God as some people do. Some people will ask of God and say, 'And if you do this for me, I promise to go to Church every Sunday.' Or, 'If you do this for me, I promise I will be good.' You must not bargain with God. The main reason for prayer is to ask for help, strength and direction and to praise and thank Him.

We are witnessing today the downfall of the Christian Church. It is being torn apart by hypocrisy. The Church is far too materialistic and is losing its credibility. It most certainly does not represent the true teachings of its founder, Jesus. The Church of England owns over three hundred thousand acres of English farmland. It has hundreds of millions of pounds in property. Its total assets amount to well over five thousand million pounds.

What was it that Jesus said? 'Do not build up treasures on earth.'

The Church of England may well be one of the richest organisations in the world, but it is spiritually bankrupt. It is time to re-educate the people. It is time for a wind of change. People must come to realise that spiritual is far more important than material, that we are all a part of God, that we are all one big happy family on the earth plane and that we must be doing all that we possibly can to help one another and to love all people everywhere.

Life on earth can be equated to a day at work. We should not be clock watching, but rather getting on with the job in hand, so that when it is our time to go home, we can pass to spirit and say, 'That was a job well done!' We can then come closer to God and be happy in the knowledge that we can now progress in spirit.

I am acting as a light in a very dark world. I am standing in a dark field, holding a candle. Those who can accept the spiritual truths that I am here to give may draw close and allow me to light their candle also. Let us work towards that day when the world can be glowing bright, shining like a light throughout the universe.

Chapter 18

Religions

Over the ages, many religions have grown up out of the world. Most of these religions have a handful of the truth within them, but I tell you this, not one religion in the world today has got it right!

The careful observer can easily distinguish the truth from the man-made dogmas and sift the wheat from the chaff. People, however, do not choose to do this. They prefer to accept blindly the doctrines of their forefathers and run like lemmings over the cliff.

Religions are man-made, and man has taken a snippet of the truth, manipulated it, adapted it and added a few of his own ideas.

There is no need for all these different religions. There is no need for people to sit around a table and make up their own laws and ideas so that the truth might suit them better.

There is one God. It does not matter what you call Him, there is one God and his laws are the same for everyone and cannot be bent. There is no need to make things complicated. It is a simple message. God the Father wants us to love Him. If we truly love God, we will also love each other. All other religious teachings take care of themselves. If you love God and therefore one another, you automatically will not kill, rape, steal etc. It is so simple, why do people try to make things complicated? Why do people fight in the name of God? What a contradiction of terms!

There is one God and you should love Him. That is the message. If you truly do this, everything else takes care of itself and there is no need to have different religions.

I do not follow any one creed. We should not follow laid down dogmas.

If these many religions could open their minds and hearts to understand that they do not hold the whole truth, then perhaps the world could take a step on the right pathway.

It is difficult to describe a religion in just a few words, because a book could be written about each one.

The religion called 'Hinduism' dates back from around AD 1200 to 1300. This was the time when the invading Muslims wished to distinguish the faith of the people of India from their own. 'Hindu' is, in fact, a Persian word for Indian. Indians themselves, however, prefer to speak of the 'Eternal Teaching' or Law.

Hinduism has no real founder and no prophets. It has no particular laid down creed. The emphasis in Hinduism is on the way of living rather than on the way of thought. It is more of a way of life or a culture than a particular creed. Not everyone who is born a Hindu is what is called a practising Hindu, but rather it is claimed that they are Hindus because they were born into the religion, rather like people in England may be called Church of

England even if they do not follow any particular faith. The Hindu religion is closely entwined with the tradition of the land of India, its social system and its history.

I find Hinduism quite a confusing religion. The inhabitants of one village may not share in the same focus of worship which will unite the villagers of another place. The vast majority of Hindus believe in God in some form or other, but there are those who do not. Some Hindus worship Sheba, others Vishnu or his incarnations, most notably Krishna or Rama. Others again are worshippers of goddesses. The individual Hindu may revere one God, a few Gods, many Gods or even none at all! They may also believe in one God and in several Gods as manifestations of him.

Some Hindus believe in Brahman. They believe that he is the creator of all things on earth, and that he is also the creator of every human act. Hinduism is one of the religions which strictly believe that each individual has to follow a path that they have been given at birth. If, however, whilst they are on this path they commit any sort of behaviour which is against their religion, for example rape, murder or theft, they believe that when the soul reincarnates, (and they do believe in reincarnation) it can then enter an animal. This is totally wrong. In this respect, the Hindus are very much misguided. But having said that, it is not an error that is a great deal to worry about.

When we are reincarnated, we do not come back as dogs, cats, horses or flowers. Animals are animals and people are people – always. You may, of course, be reincarnated as a different sex, but not a different species.

There are many levels at which Hindus preach. There are those who literally commit their lives to preaching. They are the ones who feel that their home is in the Hindu temple, where they could sit and preach all day. Preachers sit in the temple for most part of the day, and they pray in front of many portraits of the Gods and Goddesses. The main one is Brahman, then there are his followers, for example Sita, Rama, Laxman and others who many preach about.

Many Hindus who are at a high level of preaching show their love to these Gods by lighting small candles in front of their portraits. This light is supposed to show love and purity. Those who are at a high level of preaching carry out this ritual twice daily, but there are those at a lower level of preaching who only carry out the ritual maybe once or twice a week. Usually, this is within their own homes, where they have portraits of one or more of the Goddesses. They pray in much the same way as many religions, that is by putting their hands together and closing their eyes. As I have said, I do feel that this is very confusing. I wonder who, if anyone, they are praying to!

Hindus who are at a high level of preaching usually start their prayers at five o'clock in the morning. The preacher begins his day by washing himself. He enters a temple, preferably one used by the whole of the community or one that is based in his own home, and begins the preaching by lighting the Diva. He also offers food to the

Gods, which is usually in the form of fruit. After his prayers, the fruit becomes holy food and it is passed around the people, who have a little to eat. There are incense sticks which are lit in order to give the home or temple a beautiful fragrance, and the preacher, when he sits down to preach, faces the portraits of the Goddesses and reads passages from their bible which is called the Bhagavad Gita.

I suppose one of the best known Hindus in history was Gandhi. He once said, 'My life is my message!' For him, truth was God and non-violence was the way to achieve the realisation of God. His life was devoted to winning independence for India and raising the country's status. His Hinduism was all-embracing, although he respected other traditions and other religions. He did have an affection for the Bhagavad Gita. He claimed that his version of Hinduism included all that he knew to be best in Islam, Christianity, Buddhism and others. On the other hand however, his teaching cannot be understood, apart from three basic Hindu concepts which are duty, discipline of action, and spiritual deliverance.

It has been suggested that Hinduism is a federation of cults and customs. This is largely true, because Hinduism has indeed grown up out of India from old traditions and customs. Hinduism, as with most religions, has captured a sprinkling of truth, and although somewhat divided in their beliefs, they are not as misguided as many other religions, including the orthodox Christian religions.

Buddhism is another religion which contains a handful of the truth. In contrast to the last hundred years, hardly any doubt remains today that their historical Buddha, the founder of Buddhism, actually lived. His life, however, is greatly interwoven by legend, and rather than an accurate biography, tradition offers an idealised portrait of what all good Buddhists should strive to become. Nevertheless, certain facts about his life can be established fairly clearly.

Siddartha Gautama, later known as 'Buddha', was born approximately six hundred years before Christ. He was born in a village called Lumbini near the modern border between India and Nepal. As is common with the founder of any religion, all sorts of legends have grown up around his birth. In accordance with the idea of rebirth and reincarnation, these even include details of his previous existences. The story is told that during his last but one incarnation, the Buddha looked down from the heavens to find the right time, place and parents for his reincarnation. He chose a period of history where human life could last up to a hundred years, neither too long nor too short for his teachings to be grasped. As a place of birth, he chose Northern India, which was regarded as the central land. One night, the mother of Buddha, who was called Mayer, dreamed that a white elephant entered her womb, and ten months later in Lumbini on the day of the full moon in May, she bore her child. The earth trembled and supernatural beings were present at the birth. Mayer died seven days later, for she who has born a Buddha may never serve any other purpose afterwards.

That is the way the story goes, but I am unsure of the degree of credibility which can be attributed to this legend.

The name the parents chose for the boy, 'Siddharta', meant 'He who has reached his goal'. Later, as was the custom in Indian families, he chose a second name 'Gautama', after the famous Hindu teacher from whom he was descended. Buddha, the name by which he came to be known, is actually a title of honour meaning 'The Awakened One' or 'The Enlightened One'. This title became attached to his name in much the same way that the title 'Christ' became attached to the name of Jesus. Jesus's name of course was never Christ, and Siddharta Gautama's name, of course, was never Buddha.

Before Siddharta left his home for good, he made three journeys on which he was faced with life's realities in a way which he had never before known. He saw the suffering of the world in three forms; a frail old man, an invalid racked with pain and a funeral procession with weeping mourners. When he asked in amazement what all this meant, the answer was given that this was merely the common fate of all mankind. This deeply troubled him and he returned home.

Gautama was brought up as a prince and lived in a palace. He married at an early age and had one son. At the age of twenty nine however, he was driven by some inner compulsion to leave this outwardly splendid existence for the homeless life of a holy man. His decision to leave home and become homeless was evidently the result of a long felt aspiration to higher things.

Gautama took instructions from religious teachers, but apparently most of the first six or seven years after he left home was spent in religious exercises alone. These exercises became increasingly severe; for example, he fasted to the extent that the hair fell from his limbs.

He became aware of spiritual and moral futility, and adopted the quieter methods of meditation and faith. This was the specific context of his 'enlightenment'. The religious experience which was instrumental in deciding his entire later life. The Buddha began to teach shortly after his experience of enlightenment, and he soon won disciples who followed him into the homeless life and missionary service. Their way of life may be characterised as meditative. They were, in effect, a missionary order. Their teaching, however, was also aimed at ordinary men and women who did not expect to enter the monastery way of life.

The mission which Buddha evidently undertook, had no parallel in the previous religious history of India. Throughout the rest of his life, he travelled the country with his disciples, dedicated to spreading this 'liberating truth'. Buddhists believe that the world operates by natural law and power. They deny the existence of any personal God.

According to Buddhist beliefs, man is worthless as he has only a temporary existence. One of the main problems with Buddhism is the many different forms which it takes; consequently there is a wide variety of beliefs in the different sects, with much that is contradictory. Here we can draw a parallel between Hinduism and Buddhism, in that they are both families of religions rather than one single religion.

I find it remarkable that a religion (if it can be called a religion), which professes no knowledge, worships no Gods and does not believe in any supernatural person, should be followed by almost one third of the world's population.

It is true that Buddha is held in reverence, but it is not believed that he now exists. There is no prayer to Buddha, yet his name is sanctified and his teachings are as influential as ever.

The teachings of Buddha are very negative and rather depressing. They state that all individual existence is miserable and painful. In Buddha's own words, 'Earth is suffering, ageing is suffering, illness is suffering, worry, misery, pain, distress and despair are suffering. Not attaining what one desires is suffering. Everyone must be striving to be enlightened, which is the only way out of this continuous suffering. The alternative to this suffering is reaching a state called 'Nirvana'. This state may be described as nothingness. The early Buddhist scriptures described this state as follows: 'Nirvana is the area where there is no earth, water, fire and air. It is not the region of infinite space, nor that of infinite consciousness. It is not the region of nothing at all, nor the border between distinguishing and not distinguishing. Not this world, nor the other world, where there is neither sun nor moon. I will not call it coming and going nor standing still, nor fading away nor beginning. It is without foundation, without continuation and without stopping. It is the end of suffering.'

In other words, the Buddhist teaching is that we have one life after another of continuous misery and suffering until we become enlightened and then there is nothing. If this is what almost one third of the world's population believes in, I can only say that I feel very sorry for them!

Islam began in Mecca between the years AD 600 to 650.

Mohammed was born in Mecca around the year 570, and it was around the year 600 that Mohammed began to preach.

He was of the belief that he was receiving messages from God, and passed on these 'messages' to those around him.

A collection of these messages form the Qur'an. Mohammed proclaimed that God was one, known as Allah, and that he controlled the course of all events. On the last day, Allah would judge all men according to their earthly acts and deeds, and would send them either to heaven or hell. This is in fact, not far from the truth, but this man had many Jews executed simply because they opposed his beliefs!

Mohammed started out as a prophet, but because he could not get people to listen to his revelations, he soon decided he must become a military leader. In other words, Mohammed's philosophy was, 'If people don't listen to me, kill them!' This is where the expression, 'Islam, or the sword' comes from. He was not the most democratic of men!

Nothing much has changed over the years. Some Muslims today would still gladly kill anyone who disagrees with their beliefs, as has been proven in the Salman Rushdie affair. People tend to overlook God's commandment of 'Thou shalt not kill'. Even today, Muslims believe that what Mohammed preached were the actual words of God.

Mohammed originally ordered his followers to face towards Jerusalem when they prayed. This instruction is written in the Qur'an, but later when the Jewish people refused to follow Mohammed, he decided to change the direction of prayer completely, and told his followers to face towards Mecca.

Mohammed did receive some Jewish and some Christian teaching, but failed in his efforts to understand. One of Mohammed's wives was a Jewess, and another was a Christian from Ethiopia. Mohammed had difficulty in grasping these religious teachings, which accounts for much of the confusion in the Qur'an concerning the prophets and Jesus.

Chapter 19

Heaven and Hell

Why is it, I wonder, that many church leaders paint us a picture of heaven and hell that would be more fitting in a book of fairy stories?

The impression which people receive is that heaven is where everyone floats along on a cloud, playing a harp, with a halo above their head and wings on their backs! Hell is where you find a man in a red cat suit. He carries a toasting fork with which to stoke the fires!

Do certain church leaders allow us to believe this because they themselves believe that it is true, or is it just because they do not know what else to say?

There are many planes of existence in spirit, as we have established, and how you live your life here on earth determines which plane, or which dimension, your new home will be in the spirit world.

There most certainly is a heaven, the beauties of which I could not attempt to describe sufficiently in earthly words. It would be impossible for me to do it justice. Suffice to say that heaven is God's house. You could not begin to imagine the beauty, the peacefulness or the radiating, all embracing love.

Some people would have you believe that when you die, you go to heaven. This is not so. Everyone dies, everyone lives after death, but no-one goes directly to heaven. No-one is good enough, pure enough or spiritual enough to go directly to heaven. Heaven must be the aim, the target, the goal we strive to work towards. Once we have learned all our lessons, perhaps over many centuries, over many earthly lives and many existences in spirit, then we can become spiritual and pure enough to enter God's house.

Do not wait until you pass over to start learning or gaining spiritual knowledge, begin now! It is a long and difficult road which leads to heaven, but it is possible for us to start walking this road now, by living a spiritual life here on earth.

In Matthew 7 verse 13, Jesus said, 'Go in through the narrow gate, because the gate to hell is wide and the road that leads to it is easy, and there are many that travel it. But the gate to life is narrow and the way that leads to it is hard, and there are few people who find it.'

Often, Jesus refers to heaven as 'life', and to hell as the world of the 'dead'. This is a symbolic reference, of course, as Jesus proved that there is no 'death', and that life is eternal.

It is too easy to sail through life, taking the easy options, not putting yourself out for anyone, and heading for the pits. Choose the hard pathway, the difficult way which leads to heaven. It is not good enough to say, 'I have never done anyone any harm.' What a waste of a life! When you pass to spirit and your life is analysed, you will be told, 'You were not expected to do any harm.

Now, what good have you done? How have you helped? What contributions did you make to your world?' Simply not doing anyone any harm, whilst not scoring a minus point, does not score a plus point either. It is still only zero! Live each day as it if it is your last. Upon waking each morning, consider what you can do for others today. Upon sleeping each evening, think over what you have achieved that day, and promise to do better tomorrow. And do not only help your friends and family. Even thieves and murderers look after their own. Give your service to everyone that needs it. When someone asks something of you, imagine it is God who stands before you and asks, and then do it with gladness in your heart, for in helping others you are pleasing Him – and by loving all people, you are loving Him.

Jesus once said that it is easier for a camel to pass through the eye of a needle than for a rich man to enter the kingdom of heaven. People try to place various interpretations on this statement in order to make exceptions for themselves, but there are no excuses. There are no loopholes. Our priorities must not lie in the direction of material gain. There is nothing wrong with honestly acquiring money, if it is spent for the good of others. It is therefore not accumulated, and the owner is never wealthy. John Wesley once said, 'Work as hard as you can to make all the money you can, and spend as little as you can in order to give away all that you can.'

No-one should be wealthy when there are starving and needy people in the world. It says, in John 1, Chapter 3, verse 17, 'If a rich person sees his brother in need, yet closes his heart against his brother, how can he claim that he loves God? My children, our love should not be just words and talk; it must be true love, which shows itself in actions.'

It is impossible for anyone who is rich to begin to climb the stairway to heaven. Upon giving away their wealth, they may begin to learn and hopefully start to progress up that stairway to heaven. Otherwise, James 5, verse 1 puts it very eloquently, 'And now, you rich people, listen to me! Weep and wail over the miseries that are coming upon you!'

And what is hell? The pits, or what was called the world of the dead, may be referred to as hell, but hell is being in any way separated from God, or not being aware of God's love for you. Always remember – at no time, day or night, can you be where God is not. So do not try to hide from Him, do not turn your back on Him, but love Him as he loves you. If you do this, you will not be in hell. If you do not, you will be in hell. Hell is not necessarily a place you travel to, but rather a condition you can find yourself in. You do not have to die to be in hell. You can be in hell now!

This earthly life is like a game of snakes and ladders. Each time you demonstrate your love of God, by your actions to others around you, you go up the ladder, but each time you reject God by your selfish actions, you go down the snake. Where will you be at the end of the game? The ladders take you towards heaven, the snakes towards hell!

Chapter 20

The Meaning of Life

What is the meaning of life? Surely this is the greatest unanswered question of all time. Usually, the question means 'What is the reason for us having this life on earth?' But, you see, if you pick up a book from the library, open it in the centre and read the middle chapter, then you will say, 'That does not make sense. I cannot understand it!' Of course you cannot! You have to read the whole book from front to back in order to understand it, and so it is with this life. You must see the whole picture before you can understand it. This life on earth is only the middle chapter.

You see, life is a continuous circle. We are in spirit, we have a life on earth and then we pass back over to spirit. There is no death, only different levels of life, and this life on earth is very important, not to mention very precious. God has given us this life for a purpose. We must prove that we are worthy of this sacred gift of life.

Our earthly life is like a day at school. We have many lessons to learn and many experiences to go through. That is why we are here; to learn, to understand, to experience and to contribute. Everyone is special and everyone has their part to play.

The most important aspect of our life is that God has given each one of use our own free will. We do what we want to do, not what we are made to do. God wishes us all to serve Him and to live our lives in the way He wants us to, but He wishes us to do it because we choose to. It is our choice completely. There are always, throughout life, different pathways which we may take, and the decision is ours.

When we look around this world of ours, it is sometimes easy to despair. We see people experiencing pain and suffering – the weak, the disabled, the homeless and the lonely. There seems to be so much unfairness in the world, with many people having the most awful experiences, whilst others appear to want for nothing and everything seems to go so easily for them. Everything is for a purpose, and there is a purpose in everything.

People often say to me, 'I seem to make the same mistakes time and time again.' These are the same people who are experiencing difficulties and think that life is so unfair, but you see, if you take your driving test and fail, then you will have to take it again and again until you pass. If you continue to make the same mistakes, then you will keep failing. So it is with life. Experiences we go through are like tests for us. Learn by your mistakes and you will not have to go through that experience again. Fail to learn and you will have to face the same experiences again. Life is not meant to be easy. Life is for learning. How many times after having difficulties, have you said, 'That will teach me a lesson'? How very true that expression is.

There is, however, a way in which we can make life a lot easier for ourselves, and it is so simple. We can make life easier for ourselves by making life easier for other people. You don't believe me? Then try it! By helping other people, I guarantee that your own life will be much happier. That is one of God's natural laws. See what you can do to be of help to anyone and everyone around you, and do not say, 'But what can I do?'

We are only renting our space here on God's earth, and the way we pay our rent is in the contributions we make to other people. So many people in this day and age are far too materialistic. They work towards accumulating material wealth, setting their sights on big houses, cars, foreign holidays and fat bank balances. You cannot take these things with you when you pass over, but you can take spiritual knowledge, so let us get our priorities right. Let the emphasis in our world be placed more on the spiritual, less on the material.

Upon passing to spirit, it is we who are accountable for all our thoughts, words and actions whilst on earth. Everything is registered and we are personally responsible for ourselves. We cannot place the blame with anyone else, and it is always important to bear in mind that the condition we will find ourselves in after our passing very much depends on how we live our lives. Make your investments well!

Wherever I travel in the world, I hear people complaining or moaning about either their own lives or the state of the world, and I say, 'What are you doing about it?' When you see anything that you are not happy with, then you must do what you can to change it. There is much misery and unhappiness in the world. Let us see what we can do to change it. We can only change the world by first changing the minds and attitudes of people living in the world.

When we pass over to spirit, as we all will, let us be happy in the knowledge that we have done all we can to leave this world a far better place than it was when we entered it. Then you will find yourself in a far better place in the world to come.

Chapter 21

Organ Transplants

Some people are of the belief that the time of death is somehow pre-determined from the moment of birth. They use expressions like, 'When your number is up, it's time to go!' But that is not strictly true. You have free will to do as you wish. There are many ways in which you may cut short your life if you wish to do so. If you choose to smoke fifty cigarettes a day, for example, you will probably not live as long as you would if you choose not to smoke.

You understand now that we are all made up of a physical body and a spiritual body, the physical being the vehicle we use whilst here on earth. As with any vehicle, like a car, if it is well looked after and treated with respect, it will serve us well but from time to time, things go wrong which have to be put right. If there is something wrong with your car, you go to a mechanic. If there is something wrong with your body, you go to a doctor.

Should your carburettor fail, you may have to go and have a new one fitted. If your heart fails, you may need to have a new one fitted. This is the way we should look upon it. Once you can accept this principle, that your body is the vehicle, then you will accept that there is nothing at all wrong with organ transplantation or blood transfusion.

When a person 'dies', they go on to a whole new world, and leave behind their physical body, which they have no further use for. Many people refuse to give permission for an organ belonging to their deceased relative to be used. They say that they want them to be buried in one piece. I find it incomprehensible! If they do not allow the organ to give someone else the hope of life, then what happens to it? It is buried and the worms get it, or it is burnt to ashes a few days later. What a waste! If people could only realise that their loved ones have already passed over 'complete' and the body is quite irrelevant to them now. In the spirit world, they are quite whole.

I always carry a donor card, and I appeal to everyone to do the same. By allowing your organs to be used after death, you can give someone a new lease of life – a life that might otherwise be cut short.

I have been asked in the past, 'Well, if the spirit world is so marvellous, why bother prolonging life at all?' The answer is very simple. By preventing lives being cut short, we are giving them the opportunity to stay here in this school of life long enough to learn more lessons, to understand more and to contribute still more to this world. As a result, we hope they will pass over having acquired still more understanding, earning themselves a beautiful home in spirit. It is not God's will that anyone be ill. It is our duty to try and help everyone with whatever skills and power God has given us.

I have read with interest about this idea of freezing the body upon death, in the hope that one day, a cure may be found, whereupon the body may be defrosted, cured and brought back to life. I am afraid that this idea is taking things a little too far. It is not, nor ever will be, possible. Once the silver cord has been broken death occurs, and the real you, the spirit is set free to live on in a new world, but the vehicle, the body, is finished with. When the cord is actually severed, there is no way on earth that the spirit can inhabit that body to live an earthly life again.

So it is on the life supporting machines. They do a wonderful job, but once the body is brainstem dead, that is to say the spirit has left and the silver cord has been cut, there is no way that the body can be resuscitated to independent life. The spirit, the real person has gone and the machine may as well be switched off.

Everyone must understand that the body is only a shell. Just as a snail lives in its shell, we live in our bodies. It is our duty, and it is sensible to take care of them whilst we inhabit them, but the body is not the real self.

In conclusion, there is nothing at all wrong with transplanting organs. One day, you may give an organ to someone who needs it. On the other hand, one day you might just be grateful to receive one!

Chapter 22

Abortions

Human life is very precious. Who can argue with that statement? But have you ever really thought about the question of when human life actually begins?

If people were to realise that the spirit enters the body at conception and that it is actually a child in their womb, then they would begin to realise just how wicked and evil abortion is.

Today, with the latest scientific and modern technology, scientists and doctors know more and more about the nature of the unborn child, and there is no doubt that at conception, the child's sex, hair colour and even eye colouring are all determined. Even before the body develops. What they cannot, however, determine with their material methods is when the spirit is present. They will never calculate this. The physical may be measured by physical means, the spirit may not.

We are always spirit, before we are born, during our earthly life and after our earthly life. The spirit of the baby is there at conception. The baby is alive in its mother's womb, preparing for its entry into our world. No-one, not even the mother should take away the right of the baby to be born and have an earthly life by undergoing an abortion.

This denies the child an opportunity of learning vital lessons on the earth, and he or she will have to grow up and develop in spirit before he or she can have the chance again.

Some women say, 'I have the right to do as I wish with my own body!' The same argument is usually used by smokers, drug addicts or alcoholics, and my reply is 'Certainly, you are only ruining your own body.' But the case of a pregnant woman is very different. She is not merely talking about her own body, but someone else's! Once the baby has been conceived, that child is a separate person.

People make excuses for abortion, but it is true to say that by far the largest percentage of abortions carried out today are for what are termed 'social reasons'. For example, 'It would ruin my career to have a baby now,' 'I can't afford another mouth to feed,' or other such reasons.

Ah, but what about rape, possibility of handicap, or when the mother's life is in danger, I hear you say.

Thankfully, the question of the mother's life being in danger is very rare these days. Less than one per cent of all abortions are carried out for this reason. In any case, this has always been legally permissible and is nothing to do with abortion on demand.

In the rare case of pregnancy occurring as a result of rape, I do not honestly think that the added trauma of abortion directly after the ordeal of rape can be good for the mother, and in any case, it is still no excuse.

Just because the baby may be unwanted is not a good enough reason to deny the child the right to live. God gives life and only God may take it away. Even rape is no excuse. If someone, whilst you are sitting in your living room alone one evening, bursts open the door, drops a baby into your lap and runs away again, do you say, 'I will put this baby in the dustbin'? Do you say, 'I will take the kitchen knife and cut this baby's throat'? It is the same thing. If you were raped and became pregnant, you did not ask for the baby, but it is now your responsibility to take care of the child and ensure that it lives. If you think that a better home could be found for it, then by all means allow a childless couple to adopt it, but you do not kill that child.

As for handicap, there is no accurate way of assessing the full potential of a baby likely to be handicapped, and in any case, just because someone is handicapped does not surely mean that they do not have the right to live? Many people find that a handicapped child brings much love to the family. In many ways, they can teach us a lot, and remember, accidents can leave people severely handicapped, but we do not take away the victim's right to live.

Whichever way you look at it, abortion on demand has got to be wrong. I am a witness that abortion is, in fact, the killing of a child and I speak for the children that cannot speak for themselves.

I see these unfortunate children trying to communicate with their parents, but even their mothers often disown them, unaware that they have a child in spirit. I feel so sorry for them, and it makes me angry. People should realise the consequences of their actions, because if they do not realise in this life on earth, then they will be made to realise in their next life in spirit.

As life begins at conception, another process which I find quite appalling is the IVF programme. IVF stand for 'In Vitro Fertilisation' or 'in glass' fertilisation. It produces life by putting together sperm and egg in a laboratory test tube – hence the expression 'test tube babies', sometimes called conceptus, embryo or whatever name people may choose. Call it what you will, but this is certainly early human life because the parents are human.

It has to be very wrong to carry out experiments on human life. Human life has value. IVF puts lives at risk, and no-one should have the right to endanger another's life. Most test tube babies die before birth. Of all the women given IVF, only about ten per cent or ten out of every one hundred actually give birth to a baby. So ninety per cent, or ninety out of every one hundred babies, will die.

Furthermore, much embryo research is carried out, not to help the infertile, but for testing out abortion drugs or for diagnosing handicap for the purpose of destroying embryos. These researchers end lives in order to discover how to end even more lives! The price of progress!

Chapter 23

Questions and Answers

Throughout your progression through the spirit planes, it becomes evident that the more you know, the more you realise that in truth, in the scale of things, you actually know very little. New found knowledge raises new questions, and each answer raises still more questions.

People often write to me with questions, or ask me over the air, and so I decided to devote a chapter of this book to your questions and my answers. I have condensed the letters for obvious reasons and omitted the names of the enquirers. There follows a cross section of the most common questions I am asked. I hope that my answers will help you all.

Question – Dear David, what happens to babies or small children when they pass over to spirit?

Answer – These infants are looked after by what are commonly termed 'adoptive spirit parents', perhaps the child's grandmother or great grandmother. These children, even the miscarried and aborted, grow up in the spirit world, where they play, learn and develop, just as they would have done had their earthly lives not been cut short. They will play with other children and go to school to learn. They will know who their earthly parents and family are, and from time to time they will be brought to visit them.

Question – Dear David, do animals have an afterlife?

Answer – They most certainly do! Very often at public meetings, I have seen cats and dogs in spirit with their owners, and on one occasion in a large theatre, I saw a horse with a young lady! It transpired that this horse had been put to sleep a few weeks previously. Of course, I cannot pass on any messages from animals, as they do not talk to me! When you pass over to spirit, you can be reunited with your pets if you wish.

Question – Dear David, I have been married twice and both my husbands have died. Which one will I go to when I pass over?

Answer – The simple answer to this question is that you go to where the love is. If there is no love between yourself and either one or both husbands, then you will not meet up with them. If, however, there is that love bond between yourself and one, or both of them, then they may be there to greet you when you pass over.

Question – Dear David, do those in the world of spirit really have all the answers?

Answer – Most certainly not! They are people, just like yourself, with limited knowledge. They too are learning all the time, although it is probably true to say that many in spirit have a far greater understanding than when they were here on earth.

One must also bear in mind where this person is in the spirit world. Someone from the high spirit realms is far more likely to talk sense than someone from the pits, because of course, they have gained more knowledge.

Question – Dear David, I visited a medium who told me that a gentleman in spirit was with me, who only had one arm. This was my grandfather who lost an arm during the war, but it upset me to think that he still only has one arm.

Answer – Those in spirit have the ability to show themselves as they were, not as they are. This is for recognition purposes. By showing himself with one arm, you were able to identify him being your grandfather, but rest assured that now, in spirit, he is complete in every way.

Anyone who passes to spirit in anyway disabled leaves behind that disabled, physical body. Their real self is in no way disabled.

Question – Dear David, my mother passed over last year, and very often I can smell her favourite perfume in my living room. Why is this?

Answer – You will smell this perfume when your mother is there with you. Those in spirit do try to make contact with us in any way they can, and your mother is letting you know that she is there by bringing this fragrance with her when she comes to you. The next time you smell her perfume, just say, 'Hello mum, thank you for letting me know you are here.'

Question – Dear David, I went to see a fortune teller whilst on holiday. She told me that my marriage wouldn't last more than two years. This has really worried me because my husband and I are very much in love and want to be together always. I only went to see this clairvoyant for a bit of fun, but now I am so worried I can think of nothing else. My husband says to take no notice as no-one can really see into the future. What do you think? By the way, this lady used a crystal ball and the tarot cards.

Answer – My answer could be rather in-depth and complicated, but I will try to simplify it. A genuine clairvoyant can be a great deal of help to people, giving guidance and advice. People should only consult a clairvoyant as you may consult a solicitor or a doctor, not for a 'bit of fun'. Of course, the problem is, as you have found out now, there are those who profess to be clairvoyant but are not. Anyone can buy a book on how to read tarot cards, that doesn't make them clairvoyant. Clairvoyance is the psychic gift of 'seeing'. My philosophy is quite simple – if you are psychic, then you do not need to use cards, crystal ball or anything else for that matter, and if you are not psychic, then you should not be trying to do the work of a clairvoyant.

God gives us all our own free will to live our lives as we wish. Of course, we can be guided and advised by spirit, but we decide ourselves which 'pathway' we go on throughout our earthly lives. We are all personally responsible for all our actions. When we pass over to spirit, we must be accountable for what we did on earth. If you accept that, then you must believe that we make our own futures. Our life is not predetermined. A genuine clairvoyant may 'see' the pathway you are on at the moment and advise you of your future, help you through difficult periods in your life, and encourage you along the way.

Now, if you and your husband wish to be together always, there is no reason why you should not, and may God be with you both in the years to come. Next time you think of consulting a clairvoyant, do at least find a genuine one, and if in doubt, don't bother!

Question – Dear David, my husband died last year whilst abroad and I had him buried over there. Now I am wondering if I should have had him flown home because I am feeling that he is now over there and not close to me. I have no grave to visit and I can't go and talk to him. What do you feel? We were happily married for over forty years.

Answer – Wherever a person dies or is buried is quite irrelevant. Time and space are so very different in the spirit world. The body, or what happens to it on physical death, is not important. What is important is the spirit, and you can rest assured that your husband is now very close to you, and will always be. There is no need for anyone to visit graves because that is not where the real person is. On your husband's birthday or on your anniversary, or any other time for that matter, put some flowers or a plant next to his photograph. Your husband is there with you in the home, not in some cold graveyard. You can talk to him just as you used to, without leaving the house.

Question – My son, aged just sixteen, committed suicide last year. I have been told that this act was wicked in the eyes of God, and that he will be in a world of darkness for eternity. Please can you help me? I can't bear to think that my son will never be happy wherever he now is.

Answer – How awful for someone to tell you that your son has been condemned for eternity to live in a world of darkness. I will try to explain as best as I can for you to understand. Yes, it is wrong to commit suicide. As I have said, life on earth is like a day at school, we have much to learn. Committing suicide is like playing truant and going home in the middle of the morning. God, however, is a very understanding parent. When someone does something wrong, they need help, not punishment. Your son is now being helped. He didn't learn his lessons on earth, so he has to learn in the spirit world. He will learn and understand and receive the help and guidance he needs to allow him to develop and progress in spirit. Take heart that your son is in safe and loving hands, and the day will come when you can be reunited in eternal love and happiness.

Chapter 24

Ghosts & Poltergeists

Words like 'ghosts' and 'poltergeist' do tend to frighten people, but they need not if only they could come to understand what ghosts and poltergeists really are. And what is a ghost? My definition is simple. Ghosts are the spirits of people who have passed on, and now appear in a form which is visible to those still living on the earth.

However, I dislike the word 'ghost', preferring to use the term 'those in spirit'. Another word which I do not generally use is 'hauntings'. This is used when someone in spirit shows their presence at different times, to different people, but always in the same place. These are what I term as 'earthbound entities'; that is to say, someone who has passed to spirit, but because of any number of reasons they are unwilling or unable to progress in spirit, and so they wander around the earth, remaining close to one area, perhaps the place where they used to live.

You may have heard the expression 'poltergeist'. This word is derived from 'polter' meaning rattling and 'geist' meaning ghost or spirit. Poltergeist activity can be quite alarming, resulting in objects moving or cups and saucers flying through the air.

The person in spirit who instigates this often utilises whatever psychic energy is available, and poltergeist activity usually happens around one particular person, more often than not an adolescent around the ages of fourteen to seventeen. This is because around this age, youngsters can generate a lot of psychic energy. You may have heard the word 'telekinesis' (the movement of objects without physical contact). This is achieved with the use of psychic energy, which is a very real force that everyone has. Although of course, few people have telekinetic ability, those in spirit can often use psychic energy in various ways to great effect, ranging from showing themselves, to moving objects.

Wherever there is poltergeist activity or telekinesis, help should be sought from an experienced medium, as this kind of activity can be extremely frightening.

I have been called in to help where people have been very frightened by so called ghosts or poltergeists, and usually everything can be cleared up in a very short time.

Often, when people are afraid that there is 'something' in their home, they call in a priest. However well-meaning the clergyman is, it is unfortunate that he usually aggravates the situation rather than help it. They do not understand such matters and often do more harm than good. Throwing 'holy water' about does nothing to convince an earthbound spirit that it would do well to move on, instead it tends to annoy or amuse them.

If you have problems at home with anything electrical, you should call in a qualified electrician. If you have problems with your car, you should call in a qualified mechanic, and if you want to know more about the workings of spirit, you should contact a reputable medium.

Always remember that these 'ghosts' are people just like the people you may meet in the street. There is usually nothing to fear from them. They merely wish to be recognised, helped or simply to say 'hello', and when a medium is called into assist, their duty is not merely to help the family here on earth, but also to help the unfortunate, lost person in spirit to progress to where he belongs.

Chapter 25

The End of the World

Do you ever ask yourself the question, 'When will the world come to an end?' Do you believe that it will one day be destroyed? Will it be during your lifetime? Can you do anything to prevent this disaster? What did Jesus say regarding the end of the world?

'No-one knows, however, when that day and hour will come, neither the angels in heaven nor the son; the Father alone knows. The coming of the son of man will be like what happened in the time of Noah. In the days before the flood, people ate and drank, men and women married up to the very day Noah went into the ark, yet they did not realise what was happening until the flood came and swept them all away. That is how it will be when the son of man comes.'

'Be on your guard then, because you do not know what day your Lord will come. If the owner of a house knew the time when the thief would come, you can be sure that he would stay awake and not let the thief break into his house. So then, you also must be ready, because the son of man will come at an hour when you are not expecting him.'

This reading was taken from Matthew 24.

This earth of ours is God's garden. He created it and added hills and mountains, trees and flowers, seas and rivers. A beautiful place for us to live our earthly lives. Why is it that man seems hell bent on destroying what God has created? Mankind appears to be doing all it can to destroy the environment.

Nations are spending billions of pounds on weapons; nuclear, chemical and conventional, whilst half the world's population are hungry. Does this make any sense? We are all God's children; why do we fight amongst ourselves? This earth is God's beautiful creation, why do we seek to destroy it?

People must listen now to the words that come from spirit. But what if people do not listen to our words? Even if people of the world do listen, but then choose to take no notice, it is perfectly clear what will happen. They will completely blow themselves up, wipe themselves out, and I doubt the world as we know it today will see out the twenty first century. The way we are going at the moment, the destruction of our world is inevitable. The world as we know it will end.

There must always be an earth plane, however. It is the training ground, the learning place, and it is so important. If we do destroy ourselves, then what will happen? God will create a new earth plane. He will have to start all over again; he will recreate the earth, place human beings onto it, and start all over again. The human race must continue, because, as I have said, there must always be an earth plane.

The earth as we know it today, this world of ours, is now already on its second time around. Destruction of the world has happened before. We must prevent it from happening again. There was a civilisation living on this planet earth millions of years ago, before the people of this present earth plane began. There was a civilisation far more in advance technologically and scientifically than we are today. But they, in their wisdom, blew each other up. They wiped out the human race.

When you hear people talking about the lost world of 'Atlantis', they do not realise just how near to the truth they are. Legend has it that Atlantis was a country or an island out in the Atlantic. It was a civilisation unequalled before or since. It is said that it vanished in little more than a day, leaving not a trace behind, and apparently, it is buried somewhere under the Atlantic Ocean.

On the earth, there was a civilisation far more advanced than we are today. They were far more advanced scientifically and technologically, but they were certainly not a very spiritual people.

The people of the planet earth did indeed vanish. They were wiped out in little more than a day, leaving not a trace behind. Not a trace of mankind, that is. They were all wiped out.

As I have said, the people who lived in this first world were far more sophisticated scientifically than we are now, but again, man's greed and selfishness led to nation fighting nation, man fighting man, and sparked off what truly was a war to end all wars. This terrific world war, of a scale which is unimaginable to us today, lasted less than two days and succeeded in wiping out the earth's hundreds of millions of inhabitants. Those who survived the original blasts found they could not live, and walked the earth plane for some days or weeks, before finally dying a long, slow, horrible tortured death.

Is this what we want for our children and our grandchildren? If we are going to prevent history repeating itself, we must collectively turn left or right to avert impending disaster. Or do we carry straight on the way we are going which will lead to complete destruction? If there is ever to be another world war, it will have neither winners nor losers, there will be no victors – everyone will perish!

Every country should be taking an interest and discussing their views. The world is here for us all, and if it is destroyed, it will affect us all.

Countries in this world are spending billions of pounds to send men into outer space, up to the moon and to visit Mars. Man will never live on any other planet. Why are we at this time wasting so much money when there are people starving in the world?

There is much that is very wrong with the world today. Certain countries are supporting terrorist organisations throughout the world, including the IRA, and some are financing 'hit squads' throughout the world. If they do not agree with something, their answer is to blow it up! They spend vast amounts of money on making chemical weapons, which in many ways are far worse than nuclear weapons. If they could only come to their senses, and realise the wrong they are doing. What are they contributing to the world? If they could just see a glimmer of where they will end up after their time on earth, then maybe they would change their ways. I tell people the truth, but sometimes the truth hurts.

Sometimes, one needs to take nasty tasting medicine in order to be made well again. The IRA, for example, is a cowardly terrorist organisation whose members support violence and murder. Its members will go straight down to the bottomless pit of those dark grey areas when they pass over to spirit. They have much to learn. How can they hope to justify placing bombs in public areas to kill innocent people? How can they make excuses on that day when they must account for all their actions, for the heartbreak and destruction they have caused? And, if this is not sickening enough, they add to their sins by pretending that they do it all in the name of God!

I wish to speak to world leaders, let us hope that they will listen and sense will prevail. This is a beautiful world that God has created for us. Let us work together, let us collectively use our knowledge and the vast assets this world has, to make this world a happier and safer place to live in.

A few thousand years after the destruction of the previous world, God created this world. One only has to read the very first words of the bible.... 'In the beginning when God created the universe, the earth was formless and desolate. The raging ocean that covered everything was engulfed in total darkness and the power of God was moving over the water. Then God commanded, 'Let there be light,' and light appeared.

God was pleased with what he saw. Then he separated the light from darkness, and he named the light 'day' and the darkness 'night'. Evening passed and morning came, that was the first day.'

You can just imagine it. The world had completely wiped itself out and it was in total darkness. God had to get to work again to create this earth plane, because the earth is the training ground for everyone in spirit.

And now, once again, the earth is on course for destruction. Symbolically, the earth is like a runaway car on a hill, heading towards the cliff. What we are going to do about it? Do we do all we can to jump into the driver's seat and try to steer it away from disaster, or do we do nothing and let it be destroyed? I am running after that car – please join me!

Individuals may well say, 'What can I do?' Individuals must unite, and together do all in their power to prevent this impending disaster. If we all work together to spread love, peace, joy and happiness in all directions, we can leave this world in the knowledge that we have preserved God's beautiful garden for our children and our children's children to enjoy.

Chapter 26

Conclusion

People of the world are thirsting for knowledge, but are people aware that the only true knowledge is spiritual knowledge? This book contains spiritual waters to quench that thirst.

Accumulating possessions and material wealth should not be anyone's aim in life, rather they should look towards acquiring spiritual knowledge. Knowledge can be gained by experiences. Both good and bad experiences are great teachers. A combined result of all experiences is what is called the character of a person. If you take the character of anyone, it is really the sum total of what that person has gone through. You will find that misery and happiness are equal factors in the formation of that character. Good and evil have an equal share in moulding the character, and in some instances, misery is a greater teacher than happiness. In studying the vast majority of great characters the world has produced, it would be found that misery taught more than happiness, and that poverty taught them more than wealth. It would be found that blows brought out their inner fire more than praise.

We should thank God for giving us the opportunity to go through these experiences and so learn our lessons. We should thank God for our tears as well as our smiles, for our joys as well as our griefs, for our weeping and our laughter, for our curses as well as our blessings, and for our praises as well as shames. We should thank God for all things. Remember, tears shed through troubles will one day turn into pearls of wisdom. As my own spirit guide says, 'Everything for a purpose and a purpose in everything.' There is a reason why things happen, but we cannot always see the reason at the time.

Throughout our earthly lives we are daily being given many lessons to learn. But do we learn those lessons? If we can learn our lessons well, if we can learn our lessons now, it will stand us in good stead for the future.

The words of this book have been revealed to me over the course of the years. When you fill a glass with water, you have to first drink that water before you can refill the glass. So it is with spiritual truths and spiritual knowledge. You can only digest so much at a time. Once you have digested what you have been given, then you are able to digest more. The people who have not yet learned simple spiritual truths will find it impossible to digest the much greater spiritual knowledge.

The words I give you are truth. Jesus never said, 'In my opinion, this is right.' He said, 'This is the truth.' So it is that this is not my opinion of the truth, this is the truth! It is no good learning about the world to come; it is no good learning about the higher spirit planes, unless by doing so, you are shown how you should be living this life on earth that is very important. It is of the utmost importance. Get this life right first, and then you can progress. You can then learn about the higher spirit planes.

When a child begins school, he starts in the infant section, he has lessons to learn and then he gets moved up to junior school, where again he has lessons to learn before moving up to the high school. There too, he has many lessons to learn, and if anything, the lessons do not get any easier, but rather they get harder. And if a child has learned his lessons well, he can then move on to university. And so it is, we have this life on earth, but this is just the infant school. Do not worry yourselves now with lessons you will be learning on the higher spirit planes. In the infant school, you would not worry yourself about the lessons you will learn in the high school. Learn your lessons well now, and then you will progress through the highest spirit planes.

From early childhood, we are given this picture of God as an elderly gentleman with a long grey beard, sitting on a throne up in the clouds. This is very wrong. We should not be teaching our children these fairy tales. We even imagine that when we pass over to spirit, we become angels all dressed in white with wings and seated comfortably on a cloud playing a harp. Why do we give our children these false impressions?

If people can just read this book and hear our words, those people who are lost, confused, miserable, unhappy or just wondering what life is all about may find through these pages some meaning for their lives, their correct pathway which leads to happiness and contentment. Then I will see that I have been successful. However, if people read this book who are lost, confused, miserable, and unhappy and after reading it, they remain so, then I have not been successful. That is what I mean by saying that my success or failure is mirrored in the success or failure of other people.

This book carries a very important message for all people of the world. How can I expect to speak to every individual in the world? The whole reason for writing this book is to give people the opportunity of hearing this very important message. I cannot, of course, talk to every individual in the world, when I cannot speak to every individual at a public lecture! It is sometimes those I do not speak to who carry the message home with them. Remember Jesus's words, 'Blessed be they who do not see and yet believe.' This is very important.

I come with a very important message. The message that there is no death, the message of the power to heal by the Holy Spirit, the message of how people should be living their lives, the message of what life is all about. This is not just a book about life after death; it is a book about life. Life before life, life during life, life after life. We are spirit. We were, we are and we will always be. My physical body is important in as much as it is the vehicle to carry this very important message to all people of the world. Once I have accomplished this, I will no longer have any need for my physical body. Accept my words and come into the light; reject my words and stay in the dark. You have no doubt heard the expression, 'You can lead the horse to water, but you cannot make him drink.' I am leading people to the water, I cannot make them drink. You will read what I have to say, and then it is up to you whether you accept or reject it.

136

Will the Church let me have the use of their large, magnificent buildings to deliver this message? I think not! They would do the same to me as they did to Jesus. They threw him out of the churches. We have to use, today, in the twenty first century whatever media coverage we can, to get this very important message across in the time that we have.

That is why I have written this book. That is why I travel around the country, indeed the world, giving lectures and demonstrations. That is why I work on radio and that is why we must use television, newspapers and magazines to spread this message in all directions, to as many people as we possibly can. When I talk to individuals, I say to them, 'This is what you must do,' because the way things are going with most people, they are not on the right pathway. They are not going in the right direction, and I advise people on the future and what they should do.

We are now speaking to the world, we are now advising the world. We are now trying to redirect the world, but we can only do that in the minds and the wills of people. As I am writing, my own spirit guide is standing behind me. His words tell me, 'I am here helping, guiding, guarding and protecting you.' I remember these words that he first said to me over forty years ago. The main difference is that then I had to rely on those in spirit speaking to me for me to pass the words on to the recipients. People say to me now, 'You are receiving this information from someone in spirit.' My reply is, 'I *am* someone in spirit. We *are* people in spirit; we are talking to you directly.'

Each person on the earth plane will be the same person upon passing over to spirit, whether they go up and are promoted, or whether they go down and are demoted. I say this to people who come to see me after losing someone very close to them, 'Just because you can't see them doesn't mean that they are not there with you.' They are just in another dimension or in another form.

Water is liquid – you can hold it in a glass in front of you and look at it. You can see it, you can feel it. If you apply heat to that water, you speed up the vibration and it turns into steam. If you slow down the vibration, you turn the water into solid ice. Ice, water, and steam all consist of the same components, but as the vibration speeds up or slows down, they take on three entirely different attributes. Ice is solid, water is fluid and steam is gas, but they are all the same. The whole of spirit is based on this very same principle, that everything is vibration. Whether in the form you take in the spirit world or the solid form you take on the earth, you are still the same.

When it rains, the rain comes down, touches the ground and then the sun comes out. The rain turns into vapour and becomes a cloud. The cloud comes across and the rain comes down, touches the ground, then rises back up and back into cloud. A very simple process. A very simple process that we were in spirit, we came down to the earth plane and we return again to spirit.

I am acting as a signpost. I will point the right direction, but if people go into any church, they will surely become confused, because the truth does not lie in any church, temple or synagogue in the world today.

Individuals can walk into a Church and be at peace with God and talk to him. They can go into these comfortable surroundings, and there is nothing wrong with that. You may speak with God wherever you wish, whether it be in a church, a field, up a mountain or on a beach. Wherever you feel at peace with God, then there you may pray. It is when people start listening to their priests and ministers that they start to become confused, because the priests and ministers do not hold the truth. Many of them have their hearts in the right place but they are poor, misguided, unfortunate people. You do not need to go into any church to hear the truth. Hear our words from spirit. You can hear the words of spirit as we travel the world. We will always have our base in Britain, but we must travel to all corners of the world to get this very important message across. The most important message they will ever hear.

Some will listen and follow in the pathway that I am trying to show them, others will branch off in different directions and lose themselves completely. When they pass over to spirit, those who have heard the word cannot say, 'We were not told. We were not shown the way!' When they pass to spirit, spirit will say to them, 'Well, you made a right mess of that! How did you get lost? We even sent you a signpost!' I am that signpost. Whether people follow or not is another thing, and when they pass over to spirit, this is what they will be told. 'We gave you a signpost, how did you get lost?'

If anything is certain in the world today, it is that every one of us is going to die. We are all going to make that tremendous journey to spirit. Some will go up, some will go down, some will go very high and some will go to the lowest depths, but either way, we must all make this journey to spirit.

As with any journey, if you are going away on holiday for example, you would prepare for that trip. You would find out what it is like there, how to get where you want to go, and what to take with you. I am telling you what the spirit world is like. I am telling you how to get to the plane you wish to go to, and I am saying, 'Take these spiritual truths with you, for material possessions will be of no use.' Because no-one knows exactly when they will be passing over and making that journey to spirit, everyone should be preparing for it now – today! Just think for a moment. Imagine that today is your last day on the earth plane. At midnight tonight, you die. In those circumstances, I am sure that most people would reflect on their earthly life, what they have done and what they should have done.

Spend time now reflecting on your life, and perhaps list the contributions you have made to other people. By doing this exercise, it makes one think. It may not be midnight tonight when you pass over, because one day you will! One of these days will be your last day. Let us put the past behind us, but we cannot change that. The future we can change. Let us make a fresh start, because if all people in the world can unite, together we can make this world a much happier place to live. We must act now, and then we may have something left to pass down to our children – and our children's children.

Contact DAVID DREW:

email : psychicdavid@live.co.uk

facebook: (david drew psychic medium)

twitter: (davidpsychic)

website: www.daviddrew.co.uk